GPTeacher

Embracing AI in Education

Susan Selle

Selle Creative

Selle Creative

Contents

Chapter 1

Introduction

Welcome to the brave new world of education - where AI and GPT technology are creeping into classrooms and students' lives, faster than you can say "Not today, plagiarism!" Teachers and professors everywhere, you might feel like you're in a showdown between human knowledge and robotic assistance, a futuristic Wild West where students armed with AI are trying to outsmart you at every turn. But fear not, friends, for this book is your trusty sidekick in navigating this technologically advanced landscape. So, buckle up and let's embark on a journey to help you gain the skills and confidence to not just survive, but thrive in this future that is now.

Picture this: you're grading a stack of essays, and you start to notice something strange. The writing is polished and, dare I say, a bit too eloquent for the average 10th grader. Squinting cock-eyed at the paper, you wonder if little Johnny has become a modern-day Shakespeare overnight, or if there's something more to it. There have been whispers of AI-powered tools that can churn out prose with the press of a button, and it dawns on you: you've got an AI bandit on your hands.

Wondering how to keep up with the rapid advances in technology may leave you feeling disheartened or even a bit defeated, but here's the thing: you don't need to wage a war against AI. Instead, this book will help you embrace AI and GPT technology as your allies, turning potential foes into powerful friends. We're going to teach you how to guide your students towards using AI ethically and responsibly, so they're not just relying on it as a crutch, but as a tool to enhance their learning experience.

Now, I can already hear some of you protesting, "But if students use AI, how will they ever learn the material?" Excellent question, dear reader! This book is all about helping you, the educator, strike that perfect balance between technology and good old fashioned human learning. We'll dive into how you can use AI to increase productivity, creativity, and inspiration for yourself and your students, while still ensuring they develop a solid foundation in their subjects.

Think of AI as the cherry on top of the learning sundae. Your students still need to master the fundamentals - that delicious, rich ice cream - but AI can provide that extra little something that makes learning even more enjoyable and effective. By understanding and embracing AI technology, you'll be able to guide your students in using these tools in ways that complement and enhance their education, rather than hinder it.

"But how do I go about doing that?" you might wonder. Well, that's where this book comes in! We'll walk you through the ins and outs of AI and GPT, and provide practical strategies for integrating them into your classroom in ways that promote ethical and responsible use. You'll learn how to tackle AI plagiarism, help students build their critical thinking skills, and even discover how AI can be your creative partner in lesson planning and classroom management.

Just like you, I'm a firm believer in the power of education, and I know that you're not the type to just sit back and let technology take over. You want to be on the front lines, guiding your students as they navigate this unfamiliar terrain, and ensuring they develop the skills and knowledge to flourish in an increasingly tech-driven world.

So, teachers and professors, this book is for you - a lighthouse in the stormy seas of AI technology. As we journey together, we'll explore ways to keep the human touch alive in education while embracing the possibilities that AI offers. You'll find tools, tips, and techniques to help you use AI as a force for good in your classroom, empowering your students to excel while maintaining their individuality and creativity.

Throughout this book, we'll delve into case studies and examples of how other educators have successfully integrated AI and GPT technology into their classrooms, providing you with inspiration and practical ideas for your own teaching journey. You'll see that AI isn't here to replace you - it's here to enhance and elevate the incredible work you're already doing.

And let's not forget about your own professional development! As we help you become more familiar with AI, you'll gain valuable skills and knowledge that will not only make you a better educator, but also prepare you for the future of teaching. We'll explore the importance of AI literacy for both educators and students, and discuss ways to bridge the digital divide, ensuring that all students have equal access to these powerful tools.

By the time you finish this book, you'll have a newfound appreciation for AI and its potential in education. You'll see that AI and GPT technology, when used responsibly and ethically, can be a catalyst for positive change and innovation in the classroom. Rather than fearing the rise of AI, you'll be ready to harness its power to create an even brighter future for your students.

So, grab your favorite cup of coffee, tea, or other beverage of choice, and let's dive into this adventure together. We'll laugh, we'll learn, and we might even shed a tear or two, but most importantly, we'll empower you to be the best educator you can be in this ever-changing, AI-driven world.

Teachers and professors, it's time to embrace our new digital assistant. Let's join forces with this incredible technology and create a classroom environment where students can thrive, learn responsibly, and make the most of the innovative tools at their disposal. The future of education is bright, and it's waiting for you to make your mark.

Welcome to GPTeacher, your guide to harnessing AI for ethical education and creative collaboration. Let's embark on this journey together and transform the way we teach, learn, and grow. We will follow the story of a typical teacher in 2023, Ms. Key, as she unlocks what she initially sees as a Pandora's box that is the artificial intelligence explosion of the 2020s, but through curiosity, a love of learning and improving her craft, and an open mind, she finds that, in actuality, it is a treasure chest of endless possibilities waiting to be discovered.

Chapter 2

Understanding AI and GPT

Unleashing Your Inner GPT Genius

Embarking on the AI Adventure: A Journey into the Unknown

A s we venture into the AI-powered education frontier, it's crucial to acknowledge that many educators, like Ms. Key, may be hesitant or fearful of the technological unknown. But as Ms. Key discovers, embracing AI can open up a world of possibilities in the realm of teaching and learning.

Initially, Ms. Key was skeptical about AI and GPT, unsure of how they would impact her students' learning experience. However, she decided to face her fears and approach the technology with vulnerability, humor, and an open mind. Her journey began with learning the basics of AI and GPT and exploring their potential applications in the classroom.

One day, as Ms. Key was getting more acquainted with ChatGPT, she decided to try it out for a lesson plan she was preparing on the solar system. She wanted to create a fun and engaging way for her students to learn about each planet.

Feeling a little unsure but excited about the possibilities, she asked ChatGPT to generate a short paragraph describing each planet as if it were a character at a dinner party. Ms. Key thought this would be an entertaining approach that would help her students remember the unique features of each celestial body.

As she eagerly awaited the AI-generated descriptions, she was initially impressed with the results. For example, ChatGPT described Jupiter as "the boisterous uncle who always has a fascinating story to share and easily becomes the center of attention, much like Jupiter's massive size and captivating stormy appearance."

However, as she continued reading, Ms. Key stumbled upon a rather peculiar description of Uranus: "Uranus, the rebellious teenager of the group, wearing a sideways cap and sitting at the table with a slightly tilted axis, always feeling a little misunderstood due to its unconventional rotation and cold, blue-green atmosphere."

While the description was amusing, Ms. Key realized that relying solely on ChatGPT's output without a critical eye could lead to some unintentionally comical or even confusing content for her students. She couldn't help but chuckle at the thought of her students picturing Uranus as a misunderstood teenager with a sideways cap.

This funny mishap served as a valuable lesson for Ms. Key. She learned the importance of reviewing AI-generated content and adapting it to suit her educational goals. By combining her unique creativity and expertise with ChatGPT's ability to generate engaging content, she was able to create an entertaining and memorable lesson that resonated with her students.

From that moment on, Ms. Key approached her collaboration with ChatGPT with an even keener sense of discernment and a touch of humor, always remembering that AI, much like humans, can sometimes have a quirky side.

Ms. Key realized that, when used with a creative and critical approach, AI, especially GPT, could serve as a powerful tool to enhance her teaching methods and her students' learning experience. She discovered that AI could adapt to individual students' needs, providing personalized education and real-time feedback, which were impractical with traditional teaching methods. As she delved deeper into the world of AI, she also found ways it could save time and alleviate her workload, allowing her to focus on connecting with her students.

But Ms. Key's journey was not without its challenges. She grappled with concerns about the limitations and ethical implications of AI and GPT. She understood that while these tools held great promise, they also had flaws and required responsible usage. With determination and a growth mindset, Ms. Key embraced her role as a guide, teaching her students to use AI and GPT ethically and critically.

As Ms. Key's narrative unfolds throughout this chapter, we'll explore the highs and lows of her journey, showcasing her vulnerability, humor, and resilience in the face of uncertainty. We'll delve into her experiences and share valuable lessons for educators who might be hesitant or fearful of integrating AI and GPT into their classrooms.

Join us as we follow Ms. Key on her voyage into the world of AI and GPT, and witness how she transforms her classroom into a dynamic, engaging learning environment that nurtures creativity, critical thinking, and ethical use of technology. Together, we'll uncover strategies and insights that empower educators to embrace the potential of AI, shaping the next generation of learners and leaders, one classroom at a time.

Like a new and improved version of an old friend

Welcome to the fascinating world of ChatGPT! If you're new to this fantastic AI tool, fear not - you're about to embark on an exciting journey of discovery, and we're here to guide you every step of the way. With a dash of curiosity and a sprinkle of creativity, you'll soon be a GPT maestro, harnessing the power of artificial intelligence to transform the way you learn, work, and communicate.

"Okay... I've heard all the hullabaloo, but what actually is Chat-GPT?" Great question! ChatGPT is a powerful AI language model developed by OpenAI, based on the groundbreaking GPT architecture (generative pre-trained transformer – that's right, we're playing with transformers, y'all!). It's designed to understand and generate human-like text, making it an incredibly versatile tool for a wide range of applications, from writing assistance and brainstorming to learning and entertainment.

Comparison with Google Search

Before we dive into its workings, let's draw a parallel between Chat-GPT and a tool you're already familiar with - Google Search. Both ChatGPT and Google Search have been designed to help you find information and answer questions. However, there are some key similarities and differences in how they work and the way they deliver information to you.

Similarities:

- Both are powered by vast amounts of data: Google Search indexes webpages to provide you with the most relevant search results, while ChatGPT is trained on large amounts of text data from the internet to generate human-like responses.

- Both are user-friendly: Both Google Search and ChatGPT offer user-friendly interfaces that allow you to input your queries or requests easily.

Differences:

- Query and response format: With Google Search, you typically enter a keyword or a short phrase to receive a list of relevant websites. In contrast, ChatGPT allows you to engage in a more conversational manner, asking questions or making requests in full sentences. In return, ChatGPT provides a text-based response that resembles a human-written answer.

- Interaction style: Google Search serves as an information retrieval system, helping you find websites containing the information you seek. On the other hand, ChatGPT simulates a more interactive, human-like conversation. It's like having a chat with a knowledgeable friend who can answer your questions or assist with tasks.

- Versatility: While Google Search focuses on directing you to external sources of information, ChatGPT is more versatile. It can assist with a wide variety of tasks, such as generating ideas, composing text, providing summaries, and even offering creative input.

In summary, ChatGPT is an AI-powered conversational tool that shares some similarities with Google Search in terms of its data-driven foundation and user-friendly interface. However, it really sets itself apart from Google or other search engines in its human-like language responses, interactivity, and ability to drill down into the data at lightning speeds. Okay, GPT-4 sometimes feels like a picture loading on a 14.4k modem, watching it appear line by line, but that is only because GPT-3 and GPT-3.5 are so fast and GPT-4 is accessing so many more virtual neural networks. The more I explore GPT, the more my brain feels connected and engaged, ready to learn more and unleash my creativity.

GPTutorial

Ready to dive in? Let's explore the basics of using ChatGPT together, with a fun and engaging step-by-step tutorial!

Step 1: Sign up and log in

To begin your ChatGPT adventure, you'll need to sign up for an account at OpenAI's website. Don't worry, it's a quick and easy process - just follow the prompts, and you'll be up and running in no time! If you want to access GPT-4, you'll need a paid account, which as of April 2023 is $20/month. I'd advise playing around with GPT-3.5 first, as it is more robust than its predecessor, GPT-3, and faster than GPT-4, however GPT-4 can handle more complex queries, so once you master the art of the prompt, you may be ready for the latest and greatest.

a. go to chat.openai.com

b. select "sign up"

c. follow the prompts to sign up with your preferred method

d. fill in your name and birth date

e. verify your phone number

f. accept the terms and conditions

g. (optional) to disable OpenAI from saving chats and using your chats in training the AI (you can still manually save each GPT response with the click of a button, but your chat history won't be saved):

- click on the 3 dots by your account on the bottom left of the screen

- go to Settings

- next to Data Controls, click Show

- unclick "Chat History and Training"

Personally, I keep this on, as I would like the AI to learn from our conversations, and I'm not overly concerned with the privacy issues of AI accessing my chats, but I have a much lower threshold about this than others, so by all means, toggle if off if you have any security or privacy concerns in this regard. That being said, never put sensitive personal information in your chats whether you have this option turned on or off.

Step 2: Meet your new AI friend

Once you're logged in, you'll be greeted by a friendly interface, ready to welcome you to the world of ChatGPT. Think of it as your personal AI companion, eager to assist you with whatever you need. Don't be shy - say hello! I like to introduce myself, giving the elevator speech about my life so the AI can start to understand my writing style and my background experience. Again, I'm an open book and you certainly don't need to open your heart to OpenAI. You can skip the pleasantries and go straight to step 3 – GPT doesn't care about social niceties, although OpenAI co-founder Greg Brockman did use "please" in a TEDTalk demonstration of ChatGPT in April 2023, noting, "it's always good to be polite."

Step 3: Start a conversation

Now it's time to put ChatGPT to the test! Type a message into the text box and hit 'Send.' You can ask ChatGPT anything - from questions about history and science to ideas for your next creative project. The sky's the limit! If you have prompt block and aren't sure where to start, ask GPT to make some suggestions.

Step 4: Experiment and explore

As you chat with your new GPT buddy, you'll quickly discover just how versatile and powerful it can be. Try asking different types of questions or exploring various subjects. Feel free to let your imagination run wild - ChatGPT loves a good challenge! We'll get into lots of prompt ideas throughout this book, but disengage from your teacher side for a moment and get creative with questions about a hobby, a place you've always wanted to explore, or recipe ideas. The more creative you get, the more interesting and engaging the answers are.

Step 5: Refine and iterate

Like any great conversation, the key to success with ChatGPT is communication. If you don't quite get the response you were hoping for, don't be discouraged! Reframe your question, provide more context, or be more specific. It's all part of the learning process, both for you and your AI buddy. Embrace your inner 2-year-old and just keep asking why. Have a random question that's been nagging at you forever? Let your digital assistant track down an answer for you.

Step 6: Apply your newfound knowledge

Now that you've got the hang of using ChatGPT, it's time to unleash its full potential! Think about how you can apply this incredible tool to your everyday life, whether it's generating ideas, proofreading your work, or just having a bit of fun. The possibilities are endless! During Brockman's TEDTalk, he shared a captivating anecdote about a pet parent who was advised by their vet to adopt a "wait and see" approach regarding their sick dog's condition. However, the owner chose to enter the dog's blood test results into ChatGPT, which, after warning that it was not a vet, offered some hypotheses, which the pet owner took to another vet. This vet was then able to provide life-saving treatment for the dog, thanks to the information provided by Chat-GPT. However, you must also take ChatGPT's advice and citations with a grain of salt, as it does create its own information sometimes. We'll look at some of the drawbacks and pitfalls later, but for now, just have fun exploring and learning about whatever your heart desires.

And that's it - you're officially a ChatGPT pro! By following this simple tutorial, you've unlocked a world of AI-powered potential, ready to enrich your life and expand your horizons. So, what are you waiting for? Dive in, explore, and most importantly, have fun on your journey through the wonderful world of ChatGPT! To help you out, let's look at how to craft effective prompts to maximize the value of GPT's response.

Mastering Prompt Engineering - Crafting Effective Prompts with ChatGPT

Prompt engineering is a crucial aspect of getting the most out of Chat-GPT. It involves crafting your input in a way that elicits the desired response from the AI model. In this section, we'll explore strategies for creating better prompts and even how to ask ChatGPT itself to assist in enhancing your prompts.

1. Be Specific and Clear:

When crafting a prompt, ensure it is specific and clear. Vague or ambiguous prompts may lead to less relevant or less helpful responses. If you're looking for a detailed answer, make sure to ask a direct question or provide enough context for ChatGPT to generate a comprehensive response.

Example:

Less effective prompt: "Tell me about dogs."

More effective prompt: "What are the main differences between Labrador Retrievers and Golden Retrievers?"

2. Request Step-by-Step Explanations or Examples:

If you want more thorough responses, ask ChatGPT to provide step-by-step explanations or examples to support its answers. This can encourage more informative and detailed replies.

Example:

Less effective prompt: "How does photosynthesis work?"

More effective prompt: "Explain the process of photosynthesis in plants step by step."

3. Utilize GPT to Improve Your Prompts:

You can also ask ChatGPT for assistance in creating better prompts. For instance, request a list of possible questions on a specific topic or ask how to rephrase your prompt for optimal results.

Example:

Initial prompt: "How can I improve my question about global warming?"

ChatGPT's response: "To improve your question about global warming, you could be more specific by asking about the causes, effects, or potential solutions. For example, you could ask, 'What are the primary human activities contributing to global warming, and how can we mitigate their impact?'"

4. Experiment with Temperature and Max Tokens:

When using ChatGPT, you can adjust parameters like temperature and max tokens. Higher temperature values (e.g., 0.8) may result in more creative and diverse responses, while lower values (e.g., 0.2) can produce more focused and deterministic answers. Limiting max tokens can help keep responses concise.

5. Iterate and Refine:

Don't be afraid to experiment with different phrasings or approaches to a prompt. If ChatGPT's initial response isn't what you were hoping for, refine your prompt and try again. Iterating and refining prompts is a normal part of the process and can help you better understand how to communicate effectively with ChatGPT.

Mastering prompt engineering is essential to getting the most out of ChatGPT. By being specific, asking for detailed explanations, and even seeking assistance from ChatGPT in crafting better prompts, you can enhance the quality of the AI-generated responses. Remember to experiment with parameters and iterate on your prompts to optimize your experience with this powerful conversational AI tool.

Crafting Effective Prompts - 10 Examples for Maximizing Productivity and Creativity with ChatGPT

Crafting effective prompts is crucial for getting the most out of ChatGPT. In this section, we'll present 10 examples of less effective prompts and their more effective counterparts, focusing on maximizing productivity and creativity through GPT and other GPT tips.

Productivity:

Less effective prompt: "How can I be more productive?"
More effective prompt: "List five time management techniques to increase productivity during a workday."

Creativity:

Less effective prompt: "How can I be more creative?"
More effective prompt: "What are three exercises I can practice daily to enhance my creative thinking skills?"

Brainstorming:

Less effective prompt: "Tell me about brainstorming."

More effective prompt: "Explain the process of mind mapping and how it can improve brainstorming sessions."

Maintaining Focus:

Less effective prompt: "What are some tips for better focus?"

More effective prompt: "Describe four strategies to minimize distractions and maintain focus while working from home."

Writer's Block:

Less effective prompt: "How can I overcome writer's block?"

More effective prompt: "Suggest three practical techniques for overcoming writer's block and reigniting the creative writing process."

Using GPT:

Less effective prompt: "How to use GPT effectively?"

More effective prompt: "Provide five best practices for using ChatGPT to enhance research, writing, and creativity."

Goal-setting:

Less effective prompt: "Give me tips on setting goals."

More effective prompt: "Explain the SMART criteria for setting effective goals and provide an example of a well-defined personal goal."

Decision-making:

Less effective prompt: "How can I improve my decision-making?"

More effective prompt: "Outline a step-by-step process for making informed decisions and weighing the pros and cons of each option."

Stress Management:

Less effective prompt: "How to manage stress?"

More effective prompt: "Discuss three science-backed relaxation techniques to manage stress and maintain mental well-being."

Routines:

Less effective prompt: "What's a good morning routine?"

More effective prompt: "Design a morning routine that incorporates exercise, mindfulness, and healthy eating to kickstart a productive day."

In short, the difference between a less effective and a more effective prompt can significantly impact the quality of responses generated by ChatGPT. By being specific, asking for detailed information, and focusing on actionable advice, you can maximize productivity and creativity using ChatGPT as a powerful tool to support your personal and professional growth.

Navigating the AI Landscape: First Steps

As our dear Ms. Key took her first steps into the AI landscape, she realized that it was essential to start with the fundamentals. With a thirst for knowledge and a sense of adventure, she began researching AI and GPT, learning about their capabilities and potential applications in education.

AI-Powered Brainstorming and Idea Generation

Ms. Key's first stop on her AI journey was to explore AI-powered brainstorming and idea generation. She found that OpenAI's Chat-GPT could help spark her students' creativity, providing them with inspiration and guidance when they needed it most. By using GPT to generate diverse ideas for projects and assignments, her students gained a newfound appreciation for the power of collaboration between humans and AI.

In her classroom, Ms. Key encouraged her students to use GPT as a creative partner, asking it questions and seeking suggestions for various topics. She marveled at the unique and unexpected ideas that emerged, and so did her students. This experience reinforced the importance of cultivating curiosity and open-mindedness in the face of new technologies.

Example applications:

1. GPT-guided brainstorming sessions for essay topics, project ideas, or debate issues

   a. "List ten unique and engaging essay topics related to the impact of technology on society."

   b. "Generate five innovative project ideas that focus on promoting environmental sustainability."

   c. "Suggest six thought-provoking debate issues related to the ethical implications of artificial intelligence."

   d. "Provide eight essay topics that explore the intersection of culture and language."

   e. "Propose seven project ideas that encourage students to investigate the history of their local community."

2. Using AI to generate creative prompts for writing assignments or art projects

   a. "Create five imaginative story prompts that incorporate elements of magical realism."

   b. "Generate five art project ideas that use recycled materials to create a visual representation of climate change."

   c. "Suggest five writing assignments that encourage students to explore different perspectives on a global issue."

   d. "Develop five prompts for poetry assignments that focus on the theme of personal identity."

   e. "Provide five art project ideas that challenge students to use mixed media techniques to express a social issue."

3. Employing AI to suggest potential research questions or hypotheses for science experiments

   a. "List five research questions related to the effects of sleep on cognitive performance."

   b. "Suggest five hypotheses about how different types of music can influence plant growth."

   c. "Generate five research questions that investigate the relationship between nutrition and mental health."

   d. "Propose five hypotheses exploring the impact of various environmental factors on the behavior of animals."

   e. "Provide five research questions that examine the potential benefits and drawbacks of renewable energy sources."

Collaborative Writing and Editing with AI

As Ms. Key continued her exploration, she discovered the world of collaborative writing and editing with AI. She quickly recognized that GPT could enhance her students' writing, making it more engaging and polished. By using GPT as an editing assistant, her students could refine their work more efficiently, improving their writing skills in the process.

Ms. Key implemented GPT-powered writing tools in her classroom, observing as her students received real-time suggestions and corrections. She encouraged them to analyze GPT's recommendations critically, fostering their ability to evaluate the quality and relevance of AI-generated content. This approach helped her students become more discerning writers, while also making the writing process more enjoyable.

Example applications:

Integrating GPT-generated suggestions for improving sentence structure, word choice, or grammar

a. "Provide three alternative ways to rephrase the following sentence for improved clarity and impact: 'The rapidly changing climate has a profound effect on the lives of people all over the world.'"

b. "Suggest five synonyms for the word 'significant' that could be used to enhance the following sentence: 'The discovery of penicillin was a significant milestone in medical history.'"

c. "Correct any grammar, punctuation, or syntax errors in the following sentence: 'Despite it's small size, the ant can carry objects many times heavier than their own body weight.'"

d. "Revise the following sentence to make it more concise and impactful: 'In order to maintain a healthy lifestyle, it is important for people to make sure that they exercise regularly and eat a balanced diet.'"

e. "Suggest three ways to improve the following sentence's structure for better readability: 'The beautiful, majestic, and awe-inspiring sunset made everyone at the beach stop and stare in wonder at the vibrant colors of the sky.'"

Pairing students with AI to co-write stories, essays, or reports

a. "Collaborate with me to write the first paragraph of a short story about a young inventor who creates a time machine."

b. "Help me draft an introduction for an essay discussing the role of social media in shaping public opinion."

c. "Co-write with me the opening scene of a play set in a futuristic city where humans and robots coexist."

d. "Assist me in writing the first section of a report on the effects of deforestation on local ecosystems and biodiversity."

e. "Work with me to create the opening lines of a poem inspired by the beauty and power of nature."

Using AI to help students overcome writer's block or develop their writing voice

a. "I'm stuck on how to start my personal essay about my experience volunteering at a local animal shelter. Can you give me three engaging opening sentences to choose from?"

b. "I'm having trouble finding the right words to express my feelings in a letter to my future self. Can you provide some phrases or sentence structures that convey a sense of introspection and hope?"

c. "I'm writing a short story set in a dystopian world but can't think of a unique twist. Can you suggest a few unexpected plot developments that would make the story stand out?"

d. "I want to develop a distinct writing voice for my blog about sustainable living. Can you provide examples of writing styles and tones that would be engaging and informative for readers?"

e. "I'm struggling to conclude my essay on the challenges of space exploration. Can you offer three different closing sentences that effectively summarize the main points and leave a lasting impression?"

Enhancing Multimedia Projects with AI

Next, Ms. Key ventured into the realm of multimedia projects. She learned about the various ways AI could elevate her students' work, from video editing and animation to music composition. By incorporating AI tools into her classroom, she enabled her students to create impressive and immersive multimedia presentations that showcased their talents and creativity.

Ms. Key found that AI tools could help her students save time and effort in their projects, allowing them to focus on developing their skills and expressing their ideas. She also discovered that using AI in multimedia projects promoted collaboration, as students could share their AI-generated content with their peers, offering feedback and suggestions for improvement.

Example applications:

AI-generated music composition for student films or podcasts

a. "Compose a 30-second upbeat and energetic theme song with guitar tabs for a student podcast about the latest technology trends."
b. "Create a dramatic and suspenseful background score for a student film's climactic scene involving a chase sequence."
c. "Generate a calming and soothing instrumental piece to be used during a mindfulness segment in a student-led wellness podcast."
d. "Craft an inspirational and uplifting musical theme for a documentary about environmental conservation efforts."
e. "Produce a nostalgic and emotional piano composition for a student film that explores themes of loss and healing.

Using AI to create animations, infographics, or interactive visuals

a. "Design an animated infographic that illustrates the major milestones in the history of space exploration."
b. "Create a visually engaging and interactive map that displays the distribution of different animal species around the world."
c. "Develop a dynamic and colorful animation to help explain the concept of photosynthesis to elementary school students."
d. "Craft an infographic that effectively visualizes the impact of climate change on global temperatures and sea levels."
e. "Generate an interactive visualization that allows users to explore the relationships between various factors affecting public health."

Employing AI to streamline video editing or audio mixing processes

a. "Help me edit a 10-minute student film by automatically removing any shaky camera footage and improving the overall video stabilization."

b. "Suggest a way to enhance the audio quality of a podcast recording by removing background noise and adjusting the volume levels for a more balanced listening experience."

c. "Assist me in creating smooth and seamless transitions between different video clips for a student documentary about urban development."

d. "Provide guidance on how to mix and master a student-produced song by adjusting the various instrument and vocal tracks for optimal audio quality."

e. "Help me efficiently edit a lengthy interview by automatically identifying and removing any long pauses, filler words, or irrelevant content."

Building Student Creativity and Critical Thinking

With her newfound knowledge of AI and GPT, Ms. Key sought to foster a love of exploration, questioning, and innovation in her students. By using AI as a valuable tool to support their growth, she aimed to nurture their curiosity and resourcefulness, setting them up for a lifetime of confident, creative thinking.

Ms. Key introduced her students to various AI-powered learning platforms, encouraging them to experiment and take risks. She emphasized the importance of embracing challenges and learning from failure, reminding her students that AI tools could aid their growth but should never replace their hard work and dedication.

Example applications:

- AI-assisted problem-solving activities in math, science, or engineering.

- Using AI to help students develop critical thinking skills through analysis of AI-generated content.

- Incorporating AI-generated prompts in class discussions or debates to challenge students' perspectives.

Case Studies of Successful AI-Human Collaboration

To further inspire her students, Ms. Key shared stories of successful AI-human collaboration from other educators and students. These real-life case studies demonstrated the potential of AI as a creative partner, offering valuable insights into the benefits and challenges of integrating AI into the classroom.

As she shared these stories, Ms. Key encouraged her students to reflect on their own experiences with AI and GPT, discussing the lessons they had learned and the ways in which they could continue to grow as learners and innovators.

Throughout her journey, Ms. Key's vulnerability and humor served as a reminder that embracing the unknown can lead to remarkable discoveries and growth. By facing her fears and hesitations head-on, she not only broadened her own understanding of AI and GPT but also created a supportive environment for her students to thrive in this brave new world.

Empowering Educators: Tips for Embracing AI as a Creative Partner

As Ms. Key's journey progressed, she realized the importance of empowering other educators to embrace AI as a creative partner in their classrooms. She began sharing her experiences and insights, offering tips and guidance to help her fellow teachers navigate the AI landscape.

Some of her recommendations included:

- Start with the basics: Understand the fundamentals of AI and GPT before diving into specific tools and applications. This will give you a solid foundation for evaluating the quality and relevance of AI-generated content.

- Encourage critical thinking: Teach your students to question the output generated by AI tools, comparing it to their own knowledge and intuition. This will help them become more discerning consumers of AI-generated content.

- Foster digital citizenship: Promote ethical use of AI tools by teaching your students about proper citation, respecting intellectual property, and being mindful of their digital footprint.

- Cultivate a growth mindset: Emphasize the importance of embracing challenges, persevering through setbacks, and learning from failure. Remind your students that AI tools can be helpful, but they should never replace the hard work and dedication essential to personal growth and academic success.

The Future of AI in Education: Opportunities and Challenges

As Ms. Key and her students continued to explore the world of AI and GPT, they couldn't help but wonder what the future might hold. With technology constantly evolving, the possibilities for AI in education seemed limitless, from personalized learning experiences to new forms of assessment and evaluation.

However, they also recognized the potential challenges that lay ahead, such as ensuring data privacy, addressing biases in AI-generated content, and maintaining a human touch in an increasingly digital world.

By engaging in open and honest discussions about the opportunities and challenges of AI in education, Ms. Key and her students prepared themselves for a future in which AI would play an ever-expanding role in their lives, both inside and outside the classroom.

Ms. Key's journey into the world of AI and GPT serves as an inspiring example of how embracing the unknown can lead to extraordinary growth and discovery. By keeping an open mind and engaging in meaningful conversations about ethics and responsibility in the world of artificial intelligence, educators like Ms. Key can pave the way for a new era of creative collaboration between humans and AI.

With the right tools, techniques, and strategies, the possibilities for AI as a creative partner in education are truly limitless. By embracing AI and GPT with curiosity, enthusiasm, and a sense of responsibility, educators can shape the next generation of learners and leaders, one classroom at a time.

Ms. Key's Takeaways from Understanding AI and GPT in Education

Key Takeaway 1: Understand the core principles and history of AI and GPT technologies.

GPT Prompts:

a. Explain the fundamental differences between traditional algorithms and AI algorithms.

b. How has AI technology evolved over the past few decades?

c. Describe the development and improvements in GPT from GPT-1 to GPT-4.

d. What are some major milestones in the history of AI?

e. How do AI algorithms learn and improve over time?

Key Takeaway 2: The potential benefits of AI and GPT in education.

GPT Prompts:

a. How can AI and GPT support personalized learning experiences for students?

b. In what ways can AI tools assist in classroom management and administration?

c. How do AI and GPT technologies foster creativity and innovation in the classroom?

d. What are the advantages of using AI tools for assessment and feedback?

e. How can AI and GPT technologies help teachers address diverse learning needs?

Key Takeaway 3: Recognizing the limitations and potential risks of AI and GPT in education.

GPT Prompts:

a. What are some challenges that educators may face when implementing AI in the classroom?

b. How might AI technologies inadvertently reinforce biases or stereotypes?

c. What are the concerns around privacy and data security in AI-driven education?

d. How can educators manage over-reliance on AI tools by students?

e. What are some potential ethical dilemmas associated with AI in education?

Key Takeaway 4: Staying informed about the latest developments in AI and GPT technologies.

GPT Prompts:

a. What are some reliable sources of information on AI and GPT advancements?

b. How can educators participate in professional development opportunities related to AI?

c. What are the best ways for teachers to stay up-to-date on AI research and applications?

d. How can collaboration among educators help in understanding AI and GPT technologies?

e. What are some practical ways for teachers to experiment with AI tools in their classrooms?

Key Takeaway 5: Fostering an inclusive and equitable approach to AI in education.

GPT Prompts:

a. How can educators ensure that all students have equal access to AI tools and resources?

b. What are some strategies to bridge the digital divide when implementing AI in the classroom?

c. How can teachers promote a culturally responsive approach to AI in education?

d. In what ways can AI tools be used to support students with special needs?

e. How can educators involve parents and the community in AI-driven education initiatives?

Chapter 3

Combating AI Plagiarism and Encouraging Ethical Use

M s. Key, a seasoned middle school teacher, recently faced a challenging situation with her students using AI-generated content to complete their assignments. She knew that she needed to address this issue head-on and find ways to foster ethical AI use in her classroom.

To start, Ms. Key organized a class discussion to raise awareness about the importance of intellectual property and the ethical implications of using AI-generated content without proper attribution. She helped her students understand that AI-generated text should be treated with the same respect as human-authored content, and that plagiarism is unacceptable in all its forms.

She then established clear guidelines for AI use in her classroom by defining which AI applications were allowed, such as brainstorming ideas or generating rough drafts, and which were prohibited, like submitting AI-generated essays as their own work. She incorporated these guidelines into her syllabus and course materials and made sure to involve her classes in developing these rules together, creating a sense of ownership and buy-in for the students.

To encourage critical thinking and creativity, Ms. Key redesigned her assignments to make it more difficult for students to rely on AI-generated content. One such assignment required her students to research a historical event and create a multimedia presentation that incorporated different types of media, such as images, videos, and audio clips. This task required her students to engage with multiple sources and synthesize information in a unique way that AI would struggle to reproduce.

Another project involved having her students work in pairs to debate opposing sides of a controversial historical issue. This assignment encouraged critical thinking, teamwork, and the development of evidence-based arguments, which AI-generated content would find challenging to generate convincingly.

Ms. Key also emphasized the value of collaboration in her classroom. She implemented group projects and peer editing sessions to hold her students accountable to one another and foster a sense of collective responsibility for their work. By promoting a collaborative learning environment, she hoped to discourage her students from seeking shortcuts through AI-generated content.

Finally, Ms. Key reminded her students of the importance of embracing the learning process and not fixating on creating a "perfect" piece of work. She encouraged them to appreciate the unique per-

assignments that reduce AI use [handwritten marginal note]

spectives and personal touch that only they could bring to their assignments, rather than relying on AI-generated content.

In addition to addressing AI plagiarism in her own classroom, Ms. Key also shared her experiences and strategies with her fellow educators. She attended professional development workshops and collaborated with other teachers to create and share resources on ethical AI use, helping to spread the message and promote responsible AI practices in education.

By being proactive and addressing the issue of AI plagiarism head-on, Ms. Key was able to cultivate an ethical learning environment in her classroom and inspire her students to think critically, creatively, and independently. It also got her thinking about what her colleagues might want to know about this big GPT elephant in the room.

Beating the AI Bandit

First things first, we need to educate ourselves and our students about the slippery slope of plagiarism in the context of AI-generated content. You see, swiping a paragraph from a website and slapping it into an essay is a no-brainer case of plagiarism. But, when it comes to AI-generated text, the lines start to blur like an Impressionist painting. Have a heart-to-heart with your students about intellectual property and how using AI-generated content without proper attribution is just as sneaky and unacceptable as plagiarizing from a human author.

To help your students waltz through these ethical minefields, it's time to lay down the law with some crystal-clear guidelines for AI use in the classroom. Define which AI shenanigans are a-okay (e.g., using AI to brainstorm, draft outlines, or whip up rough drafts) and which are a big no-no (e.g., passing off AI-generated essays as their own work). Put these guidelines front and center in your syllabus or course materials, and bring them up like your favorite movie quote – often and with enthusiasm – to ensure your students know what's expected of them.

Now, here's a brilliant idea: design assignments that outsmart even the wiliest AI-generated responses. Encourage critical thinking, creativity, and soul-searching by assigning open-ended questions, brain-tickling problem-solving tasks, or projects that require students to draw from their own experiences and insights. By challenging your students to think beyond AI-generated text, you'll be promoting authentic learning and fostering a deeper connection to the material – you know, the kind that makes you feel all warm and fuzzy inside.

Let's explore some real-world assignment ideas for various educational levels that encourage students to think critically and creatively, making it difficult for them to rely solely on AI-generated content.

Upper Elementary:

1. Personal narrative: Have students write a story about a memorable event from their own lives, focusing on sensory details and emotions. This requires students to draw from personal experiences that AI cannot replicate.

2. Design a new invention: Encourage students to brainstorm and illustrate a new invention that solves a specific problem. They should provide a written explanation of how their invention works and why it's important.

Middle School:

1. Create a multimedia presentation: Assign students to research a topic and create a multimedia presentation that incorporates various forms of media (e.g., images, videos, audio). This will require them to engage with multiple sources and synthesize information in a unique way that AI would struggle to mimic.

2. Debate: Divide students into teams and have them research and argue different sides of a controversial issue. This encourages critical thinking and the development of strong arguments based on evidence, which AI may not be able to generate as convincingly.

High School:

1. Research paper with an original thesis: Assign a research paper where students must develop an original thesis statement and support it with evidence from multiple sources. This forces them to analyze, synthesize, and evaluate information in a way that AI would find challenging.

2. Creative writing with constraints: Provide specific constraints for a creative writing assignment, such as writing a short story with a particular setting, character, or conflict. This will push students to think outside the box and create a unique piece that an AI would struggle to generate.

College:

1. Interdisciplinary projects: Assign students to work on projects that require them to integrate knowledge from multiple disciplines. For example, they might analyze a social issue from the perspectives of history, sociology, and economics. This forces students to engage with various academic fields, making it difficult for AI to generate a comprehensive response.

2. Portfolio of work: Instead of assigning a single paper or project, have students create a portfolio of work that demonstrates their mastery of course material. This could include essays, reflections, case studies, or multimedia projects. By requiring a variety of assignments, students must engage deeply with the material, making it challenging for AI to generate all components of the portfolio.

With more and more schools and charters offering independent study options, I want to place a special focus on that area in this book, as there is a gap in the literature and resources available for these educational settings, while also providing suggestions for a variety of other levels in traditional schools like those above. That being said, here are some suggestions for outsmarting AI in an independent study setting.

Individualized curriculum for charter schools, home schools, and online curriculum platforms like Apex and StrongMind can be enhanced with independent study projects that engage students and encourage them to think beyond AI-generated content. Here are some ideas for **independent study teachers:**

1. Inquiry-based projects:

Assign students an open-ended project that requires them to explore a topic of their choice related to the curriculum. They can create a research question, investigate various sources, and present their findings in a format of their choosing (e.g., essay, video, podcast, or presentation). This promotes active learning and critical thinking, making it difficult for AI to generate the entire project.

2. Real-world problem-solving:

Have students identify a real-world issue or challenge that interests them, and then develop a solution or strategy to address it. This can involve researching the problem, brainstorming ideas, and creating an action plan. This type of project requires students to apply their knowledge and creativity, making it challenging for AI to complete.

3. Reflective journaling:

Encourage students to maintain a reflective journal throughout the course, where they record their thoughts, questions, and insights related to the material. This can help deepen their understanding and promote metacognition. Reflective writing requires students to think critically about their own learning, which is not something AI can easily generate.

4. Virtual field trips and interviews:

Assign students to virtually "visit" a relevant site, museum, or organization and gather information about a specific topic. They can also be asked to conduct an interview with an expert in the field, either online or in person. These activities require students to engage with real-world sources and apply their learning, making it difficult for AI to complete the assignment.

5. Creative arts integration:

Encourage students to integrate their learning with creative arts, such as visual arts, music, or creative writing. For example, they could create a painting or illustration that represents a concept from the course or compose a song that teaches a specific topic. Creative projects require students to think beyond the text and apply their own unique perspective, which AI would struggle to mimic.

By incorporating these independent study projects into an online curriculum, teachers can create a more engaging and personalized learning experience that encourages students to think critically and creatively, reducing their reliance on AI-generated content.

The Power of Collaboration

Don't forget about the power of teamwork and collaboration! When students are accountable to their peers, they might think twice before turning to AI-generated content for a sneaky shortcut. Encourage students to join forces on group projects or engage in peer editing sessions to foster a sense of collective responsibility and ownership over their work. After all, teamwork makes the dream work!

Lastly, let's have a little heart-to-heart about the importance of learning from mistakes and embracing the learning process, rather than obsessing over creating a "perfect" piece of work. Remind your students that while AI-generated content may seem shinier than a new penny, it often lacks the nuance, creativity, and personal touch that only human minds can bring to the table. By cultivating a classroom culture that values growth and exploration, you'll help your students see the value in doing the work themselves, instead of relying on AI as a quick-fix solution. But since we mentioned AI quick-fixes, here is a little GPT gem just for us teachers. Learning how to engineer effective prompts will not only re-energize your passion for your content area, but GPT can help you refresh your curriculum, turn lesson-planning into a flick of the wrist (or a quick speech to text, as I prefer), and help you cultivate the classroom culture you envisioned when you first started teaching.

Sample GPT Prompt: Classroom Culture

For a quick example, I entered the following prompt into ChatGPT-4 with no prior prompting in that chat session: "how can teachers use GPT or ai to help cultivate classroom culture that values growth and creativity?" The response ChatGPT came up with was mind-blowing.

GPT Response: *Teachers can harness the power of GPT and AI to cultivate a classroom culture that values growth and creativity by using these technologies to enhance learning experiences, support differentiated instruction, and encourage innovation. Here are some ways teachers can utilize AI and GPT to foster a growth-oriented and creative classroom environment:*

1. Personalized feedback: Teachers can use GPT and AI tools to provide personalized feedback on student work. By analyzing students' strengths and weaknesses, these tools can generate targeted feedback that helps students grow and improve. This encourages a growth mindset, where students see feedback as an opportunity to learn and develop their skills.

2. *Differentiated instruction:* AI can help teachers differentiate instruction by identifying students' unique learning needs and recommending tailored resources or strategies. This enables teachers to provide customized support to each student, fostering an inclusive learning environment where every student can thrive and grow.

3. *Encourage collaboration:* Use AI tools that promote collaboration, such as online discussion platforms or shared digital workspaces. These tools can help students develop essential teamwork and communication skills, as well as foster a sense of belonging and shared responsibility for learning.

4. *Stimulate creativity:* Leverage GPT and AI to spark creativity by presenting students with thought-provoking prompts or generating ideas for creative projects. For example, teachers can use GPT to generate a list of creative writing prompts, encouraging students to think outside the box and stretch their imaginations.

5. *Build a growth-oriented assessment culture:* Teachers can use AI to create assessments that focus on formative feedback and growth rather than summative scores. By using AI to analyze student progress and identify areas for improvement, teachers can develop assessments that encourage students to reflect on their learning, set goals, and work towards mastery.

6. *Model innovation:* Teachers can demonstrate the value of innovation by incorporating cutting-edge AI and GPT tools into their own teaching practice. By showcasing the creative ways they use technology to enhance learning, teachers can inspire students to embrace innovation and develop their own problem-solving skills.

7. *Encourage ethical AI use:* Teach students about the responsible and ethical use of AI and GPT technologies. By discussing the potential ben-

efits and drawbacks of these tools, teachers can foster a classroom culture that values ethical decision-making and critical thinking.

8. Foster student agency: Empower students to take charge of their learning by giving them opportunities to choose and explore AI-driven resources or tools. This sense of autonomy can motivate students to engage more deeply with their learning and develop a growth mindset.

By integrating GPT and AI technologies into the classroom in thoughtful and innovative ways, teachers can create a learning environment that promotes growth, creativity, and collaboration. Embracing these tools can help students develop essential 21st-century skills while fostering a culture that values continuous improvement and innovation.

Not too shabby, eh? If there were one or more of these that you wanted more detail on, your next prompt could be, "give me 5 real world examples for numbers 2 and 6 above." Let's see what ChatGPT says.

GPT Response: *For Number 2 (Differentiated Instruction with GPT):*

1. GPT-generated learning resources: Teachers can use GPT to create customized learning materials for students, such as short stories or articles, based on their individual reading levels, interests, and learning preferences. This ensures that each student receives tailored content that engages and challenges them.

2. GPT-based tutoring: Teachers can use GPT-powered tutoring platforms, like OpenAI's ChatGPT, to create personalized tutoring sessions for students. By analyzing their strengths, weaknesses, and progress, the platform can offer customized support, explanations, and practice questions to help each student learn at their own pace.

3. Collaborative writing projects: Teachers can use GPT to generate story prompts or ideas for collaborative writing projects that cater to students' unique interests and abilities. By assigning students to small groups based on their writing levels and interests, they can work together to develop and expand upon the generated ideas, fostering a sense of ownership and collaboration.

4. GPT-based lesson adaptations: Teachers can use GPT to adapt existing lesson plans or activities to better suit the needs of individual learners. By inputting specific information about students' learning needs, GPT can generate tailored lesson plans that address their unique challenges and strengths.

5. Self-reflection prompts: Teachers can use GPT to generate personalized self-reflection prompts for students, encouraging them to think critically about their own learning processes and growth. These prompts can be tailored to address specific learning objectives, helping students develop a growth mindset and take ownership of their learning.

For Number 6 (Model Innovation with GPT):

1. GPT-generated lesson plans: Teachers can showcase innovation by using GPT to develop creative and engaging lesson plans that incorporate new teaching methods, technologies, or interdisciplinary connections. By sharing these unique lesson plans with students, teachers can inspire them to think outside the box and embrace innovation in their own learning.

2. GPT-assisted brainstorming: Teachers can demonstrate the power of GPT by using it to generate ideas for class projects, activities, or discussions. By sharing these AI-generated ideas with students, teachers can model innovative thinking and inspire students to develop their own creative problem-solving skills.

3. GPT-powered writing feedback: Teachers can use GPT to provide real-time feedback on student writing, helping them improve their grammar, punctuation, and style. By incorporating GPT-based feedback into their own writing and lesson materials, teachers demonstrate the value of AI-driven support in the writing process.

4. GPT-generated classroom discussions: Teachers can use GPT to generate thought-provoking discussion questions or debate topics that encourage students to think critically, analyze different perspectives, and develop their communication skills. By incorporating GPT-generated questions into class discussions, teachers can model innovative teaching practices and inspire students to engage more deeply with the content.

5. GPT-assisted professional development: Teachers can model innovation by using GPT to support their own professional growth, such as generating ideas for research projects, staying up-to-date with educational trends, or identifying new teaching strategies. By sharing their experiences and successes with GPT, teachers can encourage students to embrace AI-driven tools for their own learning and personal growth.

Wow. Just wow. You are probably starting to see what a rabbit hole this can be, but in such a wonderful way! You can keep drilling down asking for more detail (and longer lists) until you get to the heart of what you are trying to figure out.

Remember when you first learned how amazing Google was? Some of you reading this may have grown up with Google, but for us Gen-Xers, it was a paradigm-shifting experience. I even remember where I was when I first learned about Google. I was working for a dotcom startup in the bubble days in the early 2000s, where the investor money, company-provided food, and innovative ideas flowed freely. After a particularly grueling foosball match, I left the employee break room and nearly slammed into Anissa, the CEO's executive assistant, who was in a bigger hurry than usual that afternoon.

"Oh my gosh, Sue," she panted, still maintaining an air of elegance through her rush, "have you heard of this thing called Google?" I speed-walked alongside her through the labyrinth of half-cubicles as she filled me in on this simplistic yet robust tool that could find you the answer to anything. There were other search engines out there, but

Google had that je ne sais quoi that turned it into a giant. ChatGPT, at least in its public infancy as I write this, reminds me so much of Google, but without having to filter search results, navigate sponsored ads, or deal with other people's crappy work.

So there you have it, my fellow educators! AI and GPT technologies present a smorgasbord of thrilling opportunities and new challenges for us to sink our teeth into. By staying informed, setting clear expectations, and promoting ethical AI use, we'll be ready to help our students navigate the twists and turns of the AI-driven world while reaping the benefits of these snazzy new tools. It's all about striking the perfect balance between embracing AI as a valuable resource and ensuring that students continue to flex their critical thinking muscles, creativity, and personal insight that make learning oh-so-meaningful.

As we move forward in this tech-infused world, it's essential to keep an open mind and adapt to the ever-changing educational landscape. But let's not lose sight of the human element that makes teaching and learning such a uniquely rewarding experience. Remember, AI is just a tool – a shiny, impressive, and sometimes bewildering tool – but it's still up to us, the compassionate and dedicated educators, to guide our students in their journey towards becoming responsible, thoughtful, and ethical users of technology.

Remember, the key to success in embracing AI and GPT technologies lies in finding that sweet spot between harnessing their incredible potential and fostering the essential human qualities that make education such a transformative experience. By striking that balance, you'll not only be empowering your students to excel in the digital age but also cultivating a generation of compassionate, critical thinkers who will continue to make this world a better place.

Addressing AI Academic Dishonesty

In this wild and wacky world that's teeming with technology and hyper-connectedness, it's no surprise that the challenges we educators face in upholding academic integrity are taking on new shapes and forms. As we embrace the mind-boggling potential of AI and GPT technology to flip our classrooms upside down and reinvent the way we teach and learn, we also have to tackle the not-so-fun reality that these tools can be misused by students to plagiarize or cheat on their work. It's up to us to make sure our classrooms stay as fabulous havens for intellectual growth, creativity, and good ol' honest learning, even in the age of AI.

The first step on this integrity-filled journey is developing a rock-solid academic integrity policy that stares down the challenges posed by AI and GPT technology. This policy needs to lay out crystal-clear expectations for students regarding the ethical and responsible use of AI tools while spelling out the consequences of crossing the line. By laying this strong foundation in our classrooms, we can help students grasp that learning is more than just racking up high grades or breezing through assignments—it's about engaging with the material, flexing those critical thinking muscles, and blossoming into well-rounded individuals.

To develop an academic integrity policy that's both effective and relevant, we teachers and educators need to get up close and personal with the capabilities and limitations of AI and GPT technology. This means getting the lowdown on how students might misuse these tools to plagiarize and being savvy about the strategies and tools we can use to detect and prevent such sneaky academic dishonesty. With this knowledge in our back pockets, we can craft policies that tackle these issues head-on and inspire students to use AI technology responsibly.

But, let's be real: creating a policy and crossing our fingers won't cut it. To truly cultivate a culture of honesty and responsibility in our classrooms, we've got to roll up our sleeves and actively instill these values in our students. This starts with practicing what we preach—being ethical and transparent in our own teaching. By showing off the right way to use AI and GPT technology in our lesson planning, instruction, and assessment, we can give students a front-row seat to the benefits of using these tools ethically and responsibly.

Plus, it's time to encourage some good old-fashioned chit-chat about academic integrity. Let's chat up the importance of honesty, hard work, and taking responsibility for our own learning. By creating an environment where students feel cozy discussing their concerns, asking questions, and seeking guidance, we can help them wrap their heads around the consequences of their actions and the value of sticking to academic integrity.

And let's not forget—educators can also whip up strategies to minimize the chances for academic dishonesty. How about designing assignments that call for critical thinking, creativity, and personal reflection? These tasks are less likely to fall victim to AI-generated plagiarism. By giving students engaging and meaningful learning experiences, we can help them see the value in doing their own work and taking pride in their intellectual growth.

At the end of the day, nurturing a culture of honesty and responsibility in the age of AI is a complex and ongoing dance. It takes the dedication and commitment of educators, students, and administrators alike. By developing a robust academic integrity policy, actively promoting ethical behavior, and adapting our teaching practices to tackle the challenges posed by AI and GPT technology, we can make sure our classrooms stay as spaces where students can learn, grow, and thrive with honesty and responsibility as their guiding stars.

Fostering a Culture of Ethics

Fostering a culture of honesty and responsibility in our classrooms is more than just a passing fancy—it's the secret sauce that helps students grow into responsible, ethical learners and global citizens. So, how can we, as educators, create an environment where honesty and responsibility reign supreme, even in a world teeming with AI and GPT technology?

First off, let's dive headfirst into building strong relationships with our students. When we take the time to genuinely connect with them and understand their needs, motivations, and struggles, we're better equipped to guide them toward embracing ethical behavior. By showing that we care about their well-being and personal growth, we can cultivate trust and encourage them to come forward with concerns, questions, or even admissions of academic dishonesty.

Next up, be sure to show some praise and recognition for honest and responsible behavior. When we give kudos to students who demonstrate integrity, we're sending a powerful message that these values are important and worth striving for. So, let's make it a point to celebrate those small wins, whether it's a student owning up to a mistake, citing sources correctly, or using AI tools responsibly.

Another fabulous strategy is to weave discussions about ethics, honesty, and responsibility into our everyday teaching. We can infuse these topics into our lesson plans and activities, engaging students in conversations about the role of AI in education, the importance of academic integrity, and the consequences of plagiarism. By providing a safe space for open dialogue, we can help students internalize these values and feel more accountable for their actions.

Don't forget to offer support and resources for students to navigate the ethical use of AI and GPT technology. We can provide clear guidelines and examples of appropriate use, as well as direct students to reliable sources and tools they can use without crossing the line. By empowering students with knowledge and resources, we can help them make informed decisions and avoid the pitfalls of academic dishonesty.

Finally, let's loop in parents and guardians in our mission to foster a culture of honesty and responsibility. By keeping them in the loop about our academic integrity policies, expectations, and the role of AI in education, we can create a united front in guiding students toward ethical behavior. When the entire school community is invested in promoting academic integrity, we're setting the stage for a culture of honesty and responsibility that reaches beyond the classroom walls.

As we embrace AI and GPT technology in our teaching and learning, it's crucial that we remain vigilant in maintaining a culture of honesty and responsibility in our classrooms. Combatting AI plagiarism and fostering a culture of integrity takes dedication, creativity, and adaptability from educators, students, and the entire school community.

By developing robust academic integrity policies, creating an environment of trust and open dialogue, celebrating honest behavior, and engaging students in conversations about ethics and responsibility, we can help them grow into ethical learners who use AI tools responsibly. As we navigate this brave new world of AI and GPT technology, let's remember that our ultimate goal is to nurture students who are not just academically successful but also honest, responsible, and ethical global citizens. Together, we can make sure that our classrooms remain vibrant spaces for authentic learning, growth, and creativity, even in the age of AI.

Embracing AI as a Creative Partner

When Ms. Key first encountered GPT, she saw it as a formidable threat to student learning, a harbinger of a new wave of plagiarism, and a potential disruptor to the educational landscape. Understandably, she was concerned about the impact this technology could have on her students and the integrity of her classroom.

However, rather than succumbing to fear and avoidance, Ms. Key chose to approach AI with an open mind. She delved into understanding the capabilities and possibilities of GPT and sought to find ways to incorporate it responsibly into her teaching practice. By engaging her students in meaningful and relevant conversations about ethics and the role of AI in their education, she was able to transform the way they approached AI-generated content.

Through her journey, Ms. Key's perspective shifted from one of apprehension to embracing AI as a creative partner. She realized that, when used ethically and mindfully, AI could enhance the educational experience and empower her students to explore new avenues of creativity and critical thinking.

Incorporating AI into her curriculum not only allowed Ms. Key to revitalize her teaching methods but also provided her students with the tools to navigate the rapidly evolving world of artificial intelligence. By fostering a classroom environment that prioritized ethical AI use, critical thinking, and collaboration, Ms. Key helped her students develop the skills and values they would need to become responsible digital citizens.

As educators, it is essential that we, too, embrace this shift in perspective and approach AI with curiosity, openness, and a sense of responsibility. By doing so, we can harness the potential of AI to enrich our classrooms, engage our students, and prepare them for a future in which technology will continue to shape the way we live, work, and learn.

Ms. Key's Takeaways from Combating AI Plagiarism and Encouraging Ethical Use

Key Takeaway 1: Importance of integrating AI ethics into the curriculum.

GPT Prompts:

a. How can educators create lesson plans that incorporate AI ethics across different subject areas?

b. What are some engaging activities that help students explore ethical dilemmas related to AI technologies?

c. How can teachers encourage critical thinking and ethical decision-making skills in the context of AI?

d. In what ways can educators collaborate with colleagues to develop AI ethics-focused learning materials?

e. How can AI ethics be integrated into existing school curricula and standards?

Key Takeaway 2: Fostering ethical decision-making skills in students.

GPT Prompts:

a. How can educators help students recognize and analyze ethical dilemmas in AI applications?

b. What are some strategies for teaching students to consider the potential consequences of AI-driven decisions?

c. How can teachers encourage empathy and perspective-taking when discussing AI ethics?

d. In what ways can educators promote a culture of responsibility and accountability around AI use?

e. How can teachers guide students in balancing ethical considerations with technological advancements?

Key Takeaway 3: Encouraging critical thinking and reflection on AI and its implications.

GPT Prompts:

a. How can educators facilitate classroom discussions that challenge students to think critically about AI technologies?

b. What are some examples of thought-provoking questions related to AI ethics that educators can use to spark debate and reflection?

c. How can teachers support students in developing their own informed opinions about AI and its potential consequences?

d. In what ways can educators create opportunities for students to engage with real-world AI ethical dilemmas?

e. How can teachers help students understand the complex interplay between AI technologies, society, and individual decision-making?

Key Takeaway 4: Preparing students for responsible AI use in their personal and professional lives.

GPT Prompts:

a. How can educators help students develop responsible habits when using AI tools outside of the classroom?

b. What are some ways teachers can guide students in making ethical choices when interacting with AI technologies in their daily lives?

c. How can educators prepare students to navigate the ethical challenges that may arise in AI-driven workplaces?

d. In what ways can teachers support students in becoming responsible digital citizens in an AI-driven world?

e. How can educators foster a commitment to lifelong learning and ethical reflection in the context of AI?

Key Takeaway 5: Promoting collaboration and open dialogue around AI ethics.

GPT Prompts:

a. How can educators create a classroom environment that encourages open dialogue and respectful debate on AI ethics?

b. What are some strategies for engaging parents and community members in discussions about AI and its ethical implications?

c. How can teachers collaborate with colleagues and experts to stay informed about AI ethics and best practices?

d. In what ways can educators participate in professional networks and communities focused on AI ethics in education?

e. How can schools and educational institutions promote a culture of ethical AI use at the organizational level?

Chapter 4

Teaching AI Ethics at All Levels - A GPT Walk-through in Drilling Down

A s Ms. Key and her friends gathered around a table in a cozy tapas bar, they were all eager to share their experiences and thoughts about AI in the classroom. Amidst the laughter, clinking glasses, and delicious bites, the conversation took a more serious turn when they began discussing the ethical implications of AI use. All four friends - Ms. Key, Mr. Smith, Ms. Johnson, and Ms. Martinez - were passionate educators who wanted the best for their students.

Ms. Key, who had recently started incorporating AI tools like Chat-GPT into her lessons, was eager to understand how she could teach her students to use AI responsibly and ethically. She shared her initial successes with using AI to help her students brainstorm ideas and receive real-time feedback on their writing assignments. However, she admitted that she was concerned about potential ethical issues that might arise as AI became more prevalent in education.

Mr. Smith, a history teacher, nodded in agreement. He shared an example of how AI had been used to create deepfake videos, which could be used to spread misinformation and manipulate public opinion. He emphasized the importance of teaching students to be critical consumers of AI-generated content and understanding the potential ethical implications of its misuse.

Ms. Johnson, a science teacher, chimed in, explaining that she had faced challenges related to data privacy and algorithmic bias in her own classroom. She described how an AI-powered learning platform had inadvertently revealed sensitive information about a student's performance to their peers, raising concerns about privacy and confidentiality. She also mentioned that the same platform had demonstrated biased behavior, favoring certain students based on factors unrelated to their academic abilities.

The conversation shifted to the need for an AI ethics curriculum. Ms. Martinez, an art teacher, expressed her enthusiasm for this idea, saying that ethical considerations should be woven into every aspect of AI use in the classroom. She suggested that educators could collaborate to develop lessons and activities focused on helping students understand the ethical dimensions of AI, such as transparency, fairness, accountability, and the broader social implications of AI adoption.

Ms. Key, feeling inspired, proposed that they use real-life case studies in their curriculum to provide students with concrete examples of AI ethical dilemmas. By analyzing situations where AI tools had caused unintended harm or perpetuated biases, she believed that stu-

dents would gain a deeper understanding of the potential consequences of AI and the importance of ethical decision-making.

The other teachers agreed, and they began brainstorming examples from various fields, such as healthcare, criminal justice, and even
entertainment. Mr. Smith mentioned a case where AI facial recognition technology had misidentified an innocent person as a criminal,
highlighting the importance of AI accuracy and the potential harms
of biased algorithms.

As they discussed these case studies, Ms. Johnson emphasized the
importance of fostering ethical decision-making skills in students. She
suggested that they could encourage students to ask critical questions,
consider multiple perspectives, and weigh the potential risks and benefits of AI use in various contexts. Through class discussions, debates,
and reflection exercises, she believed that students would develop the
ability to think critically about AI and its ethical implications.

Ms. Martinez proposed that they could further engage their students by encouraging them to lead their own AI projects, ensuring
that ethical considerations were woven into each project from the
start. She shared an example of a student who had created an AI-powered art installation that addressed issues of environmental sustainability and social justice. By allowing students to explore AI applications in areas that interested them, Ms. Martinez felt that they would
not only become skilled AI users but also ethical and responsible AI
practitioners.

As the evening progressed, the four friends continued to discuss the
many ways they could integrate AI ethics into their classrooms. They
exchanged ideas, shared resources, and made plans to collaborate on
developing an AI ethics curriculum that would benefit their students
and their community.

As they savored the last bites of tapas and sipped their drinks, Ms. Key and her friends felt a renewed sense of purpose and excitement about the potential of AI in their classrooms. They knew that by working together to teach responsible and ethical AI use, they could empower their students to become thoughtful, engaged, and ethical citizens in an increasingly AI-driven world.

The conversation that evening inspired each of them to take action in their own classrooms. Ms. Key began by addressing the ethical implications of AI in her lessons, prompting her students to consider potential biases and privacy concerns when using AI tools. She also made a conscious effort to discuss the broader social implications of AI adoption, helping her students see the larger picture and understand the impact of their decisions.

In his history classes, Mr. Smith dedicated time to discussing AI-generated deepfake videos and the risks they posed to spreading misinformation. He encouraged his students to critically evaluate the authenticity of media content and consider the ethical implications of using AI for manipulation.

Ms. Johnson, in her science classroom, focused on data privacy and algorithmic bias. She used case studies to demonstrate the real-world consequences of AI misuse and fostered discussions on how students could ensure fairness and protect privacy when using AI tools.

Ms. Martinez, always eager to incorporate creativity into her art lessons, encouraged her students to explore AI-powered art projects with ethical considerations at their core. She guided her students in identifying ethical issues related to their projects and helped them develop strategies to address these concerns.

As each of the educators implemented these changes, they continued to collaborate and share their experiences, refining their AI ethics curriculum over time. They found that by teaching responsible and ethical AI use, their students not only gained a deeper understanding of the technology but also developed the critical thinking skills necessary to navigate the complex ethical landscape surrounding AI.

In the end, Ms. Key and her friends learned that embracing AI in the classroom wasn't just about harnessing its potential to enhance learning outcomes. It was also about preparing their students for a future where AI would play an increasingly significant role in their personal and professional lives. By equipping their students with the skills to think critically about AI and make ethical decisions, these dedicated educators were shaping the next generation of responsible AI users and leaders, one conversation and classroom at a time.

Grade Level Ideas

Here's a look at some possible ways to approach this in various educational settings.

Elementary Level:

1. Begin by introducing AI concepts through age-appropriate stories and examples, such as AI-powered toys or voice assistants.

2. Discuss the importance of treating AI-powered devices and software with respect and understanding their limitations.

3. Use activities that demonstrate fairness, such as sharing toys or taking turns, to explain the concept of algorithmic bias and the importance of fairness in AI.

4. Guide students through simple AI projects, emphasizing the responsible use of tools and the importance of considering the impact of their projects on others.

5. Encourage parent involvement by sending home newsletters or hosting family workshops to educate parents about AI and how they can support their children's ethical AI use.

Middle School:

1. Use age-appropriate examples to introduce AI concepts and ethical considerations, such as chatbots, image recognition software, and recommendation algorithms.

2. Engage students in discussions about the potential biases and privacy concerns associated with AI technology.

3. Incorporate activities that demonstrate algorithmic bias and ethical decision-making, such as designing fair games or creating inclusive AI projects.

4. Encourage students to explore AI applications in various subjects, emphasizing the importance of ethical considerations in each context.

5. Host a school-wide AI ethics day or week, featuring guest speakers, workshops, and activities to promote responsible AI use among students.

High School:

1. Facilitate deeper discussions about AI ethics and potential societal implications, including job displacement, surveillance, and data privacy.

2. Use case studies to explore real-world examples of AI misuse and the consequences of unethical AI use.

3. Encourage students to take on research projects or write essays examining AI ethics and responsible use in various fields.

4. Offer elective courses or workshops on AI ethics, covering topics like algorithmic fairness, transparency, and accountability.

5. Organize AI ethics competitions or hackathons, where students develop AI-driven projects with ethical considerations at their core.

College:

1. Offer interdisciplinary courses on AI ethics, exploring the philosophical, legal, and social implications of AI use.

2. Encourage students to conduct independent research on AI ethics,

focusing on specific industries or applications.

3. Partner with AI companies or organizations to create internships or experiential learning opportunities focused on ethical AI development.

4. Organize conferences, seminars, or panel discussions featuring AI ethics experts and practitioners.

5. Create AI ethics clubs or initiatives on campus to engage students in discussions and activities related to responsible AI use.

Independent Study Settings:

1. Use online resources, such as articles, videos, and podcasts, to explore various aspects of AI ethics and responsible use.

2. Join online forums, discussion groups, or social media communities to engage with others interested in AI ethics.

3. Attend virtual conferences, webinars, or workshops on AI ethics, offered by educational institutions or industry organizations.

4. Participate in AI ethics competitions or online hackathons to apply your knowledge and collaborate with others.

5. Create a personal project, blog, or podcast to document your learning journey and share your insights on AI ethics and responsible use with a broader audience.

A GPT Walk-through

When in doubt or unsure how to approach this with your kiddos, ask GPT to make recommendations! Here is a sample prompt I entered and the real response from ChatGPT-4. "Give me a month's worth of weekly 15 minute lessons for online middle school students about using AI responsibly and ethically."

GPT's response:

Week 1: Introduction to AI and Responsible Use

Lesson 1: What is AI?

- Introduce the concept of AI and give examples of AI in everyday life.

- Discuss the roles AI plays in various industries.

- Engage students in a discussion about the benefits and challenges of AI.

Lesson 2: Understanding AI Limitations

- Explain that AI systems have biases and make mistakes.

- Discuss examples of AI limitations, such as misinterpreting data or producing inappropriate content.

- Encourage students to think critically about the information generated by AI tools.

Lesson 3: Privacy and AI

- Introduce the concept of data privacy and how it relates to AI technology.

- Discuss potential privacy concerns with AI applications, such as facial recognition and data collection.

- Teach students the importance of protecting their personal information when using AI tools.

Lesson 4: Responsible AI Use

- Discuss ways students can use AI responsibly, such as citing sources properly and respecting intellectual property.

- Encourage students to be aware of their digital footprint when using AI tools.

- Share strategies for safe and responsible online behavior.

Week 2: AI Ethics and Decision-Making

Lesson 1: What is AI Ethics?

- Introduce the concept of AI ethics and why it is important.

- Discuss key principles of AI ethics, such as fairness, transparency, and accountability.

- Encourage students to consider how these principles apply to AI use.

Lesson 2: Algorithmic Bias

- *Explain the concept of algorithmic bias and how it can lead to unfair outcomes.*

- *Share examples of real-world cases where AI systems have displayed bias.*

- *Engage students in a discussion about the importance of fairness in AI technology.*

Lesson 3: Ethical Dilemmas in AI

- *Present students with hypothetical ethical dilemmas related to AI use.*

- *Facilitate a group discussion, encouraging students to weigh the pros and cons of different actions.*

- *Teach students strategies for ethical decision-making in AI contexts.*

Lesson 4: AI and Social Impact

- *Discuss the potential social impacts of AI, such as job displacement and digital divide.*

- *Encourage students to consider the implications of AI use on society as a whole.*

- *Engage students in a discussion about the role of AI developers and users in minimizing negative impacts.*

Week 3: AI in Action - Exploring Ethical AI Applications

Lesson 1: AI for Good

- *Introduce examples of AI being used for social good, such as environmental protection, healthcare, and disaster relief.*

- *Discuss the ethical considerations behind these applications.*

- *Encourage students to think about how they might use AI to address social issues.*

Lesson 2: Bias Detection and Fair AI

- *Explore tools and techniques for detecting and mitigating algorithmic bias.*

- Discuss the importance of diverse data and inclusive algorithms in creating fair AI systems.

- Engage students in activities that demonstrate the impact of biased data on AI outcomes.

Lesson 3: AI Transparency and Accountability

- Discuss the importance of transparency and accountability in AI development and use.

- Explore techniques for increasing AI explainability and understanding how AI systems make decisions.

- Encourage students to consider the role of developers, users, and policymakers in ensuring AI transparency and accountability.

Lesson 4: Ethical AI Design

- Introduce principles of ethical AI design, such as user-centered design and value-sensitive design.

- Discuss how these principles can guide the development of AI applications that consider ethical implications.

- Engage students in a hands-on activity to design an ethical AI solution for a real-world problem.

Week 4: Becoming AI Ethics Ambassadors

Lesson 1: Promoting Responsible AI Use

- Discuss ways students can advocate for responsible AI use in their school and community.

- Encourage students to share their knowledge with peers and family members about AI ethics.

- Explore opportunities for students to participate in AI-related events or clubs to further their understanding of responsible AI use.

Lesson 2: Critical Thinking and AI

- Reinforce the importance of critical thinking when interacting with AI-generated content.

- Share strategies for evaluating the credibility and reliability of AI-generated information.

- Engage students in activities that challenge them to apply critical thinking skills when evaluating AI-generated content.

Lesson 3: Ethical AI in Creative Projects

- Encourage students to incorporate ethical AI considerations into their creative projects, such as art, writing, or programming.

- Discuss ways to ensure AI-generated content is used responsibly and ethically in their work.

- Showcase examples of creative projects that successfully integrate AI while adhering to ethical principles.

Lesson 4: Reflecting on AI Ethics Education

- Facilitate a group discussion for students to reflect on their learning about AI ethics and responsible use.

- Ask students to share their key takeaways and how they plan to apply these lessons in their future interactions with AI.

- Encourage students to continue exploring AI ethics and staying informed about the latest developments in AI technology.

By the end of this month-long series of lessons, middle school students should have a solid foundation in understanding AI ethics, recognizing the importance of responsible AI use, and applying ethical decision-making skills in various contexts. This will empower them to become informed and responsible users of AI technology as they continue their education and enter the workforce.

Pro-tip: OpenAI's ChatGPT can produce answers this long from one prompt, but it has to stop part way through. If you notice your answer andisn't complete or it stopped mid-sentence, simply type "continue" and it will pick up where it left off.

As you can see, one well-crafted prompt can save you hours of planning, but what if you are like I was a couple months ago and don't know enough about this topic to plan a lesson around this outline? That's where drilling down comes in. My next prompt in this inquiry goes like this, "That's great! Unfortunately, I don't really know much about this topic. Can you act as a teacher who specializes in teaching this topic to middle schoolers and give me a detailed lesson plan with a suggested script for the first lesson?" I like using more natural language like this, as I feel it helps teach the AI my style and it feels more like a conversation with a wise mentor for whom no question is too trivial and from whom there is always more to learn. So what was GPT's response to my vulnerable plea?

GPT response:

Lesson 1: Introduction to AI Ethics and Responsible Use

Objective:

- Students will understand the concept of AI ethics and the importance of using AI responsibly.

- Students will learn about potential ethical dilemmas related to AI.

Materials:

- Presentation slides

- Examples of AI-generated content

- Handout with AI-related ethical scenarios

Suggested Script:

1. Introduction (2 minutes)

- "Good morning/afternoon, students! Today, we are going to start an exciting new topic – AI ethics and responsible use. We will explore the importance of using AI technology in a responsible and ethical manner. As we progress through this series of lessons, we'll be examining real-life examples and discussing potential ethical dilemmas."

2. What is AI? (2 minutes)

- "Before we dive into AI ethics, let's first remind ourselves what AI is. AI, or Artificial Intelligence, refers to computer systems that can perform

tasks that usually require human intelligence, such as problem-solving, language understanding, and learning. AI is becoming increasingly present in our lives, from virtual assistants like Siri and Alexa to self-driving cars and even AI-generated art."

3. AI Ethics and Responsible Use (3 minutes)

- "Now that we know what AI is, let's talk about AI ethics. AI ethics deals with the moral values and principles that guide the development and use of AI technology. It's important to use AI responsibly because it can have a significant impact on people's lives, society, and the environment."

- "When we talk about responsible AI use, we are referring to using AI in a way that is ethical, legal, and respects the rights and well-being of individuals and communities. Some examples of responsible AI use include protecting privacy, ensuring fairness and equality, and considering the environmental impact of AI technology."

4. AI Ethical Dilemmas (5 minutes)

- "AI can sometimes lead to ethical dilemmas or situations where the right course of action is not immediately clear. I'll share some examples of AI-generated content with you. Let's take a moment to discuss the potential ethical issues that might arise in each case."

- [Present examples of AI-generated content: deepfakes, AI-generated news articles, AI-generated artwork, etc.]

- "As you can see, there are many potential ethical issues related to AI. Some common concerns include privacy, fairness, accountability, and transparency."

5. AI-related Ethical Scenarios (3 minutes)

- "Now, I'd like to give each of you a handout with a few AI-related ethical scenarios. Take a few minutes to read through the scenarios and think about the ethical issues involved. We'll discuss these scenarios as a class in our next lesson."

- [Distribute the handout with AI-related ethical scenarios.]

6. Closing (1 minute)

- "Great job today, everyone! We've just begun to scratch the surface of AI ethics and responsible use. Over the next few weeks, we'll continue exploring this topic and learning how to make informed, ethical decisions when using AI technology. Remember to review the ethical scenarios on your handout, and be prepared to discuss them in our next lesson. Have a great day!"

This lesson plan provides a suggested script and structure for the first 15-minute lesson on AI ethics and responsible use for middle school students. Adjust the script and examples as needed to better suit your specific students' needs and interests.

Having all I need to plan a robust lesson around, I now have time to go down more of a GPT rabbit hole, asking the next question that comes to mind in this realm, "what do you, dear ChatGPT, feel are the ethical considerations in citing you as a source in generating ideas and examples for my book on using GPT technology in education?" Because what's a conversation with an AI bot if we don't get a little metacognitive, right?! Here's what GPT had to say.

GPT response: *As an AI language model, I don't have personal feelings or opinions, but I can provide some guidance on the ethical considerations of citing ChatGPT in your book. Here are a few points to keep in mind:*

1. Transparency: Clearly acknowledge the use of ChatGPT in generating ideas and examples in your book. This helps maintain transparency and allows readers to understand the origin of the content.

2. Attribution: While ChatGPT is an AI model and not an individual, it's still important to provide appropriate attribution to the technology. You may want to credit OpenAI, the organization responsible for developing and maintaining the ChatGPT model.

3. Limitations and biases: Be aware of the limitations and potential biases of AI-generated content, and inform your readers about them. AI models like ChatGPT are trained on vast amounts of text data, which may contain biases or inaccuracies. Acknowledge these limitations and encourage critical thinking and verification of the information provided.

4. Responsible use: Make sure that you use ChatGPT-generated content responsibly and ethically. Avoid using AI-generated content in a way that may harm individuals, communities, or the environment.

5. Intellectual property: Ensure that any AI-generated content does not infringe on the intellectual property rights of others. For instance, if ChatGPT generates content that closely resembles existing copyrighted material, it's essential to avoid using it in your book.

By considering these ethical aspects when citing ChatGPT as a source in your book, you can help promote responsible and ethical use of AI technology in the field of education.

Fair points, GPT! Which brings me to my next prompt: "AI-assisted authorship is a new realm and I don't really know how to describe it. I've written the bulk of the book myself, but used lists generated by ChatGPT as well as cited examples of actual ChatGPT responses. Please provide 10 different creative ways to describe this AI-human collaboration to my readers and on the cover of my book." I know I'm taking a personal tangent away from education for a moment, but hopefully walking through my thought process and interactions with GPT will help you not only understand how I used GPT as a creative partner, but also how random you can get with questions and prompts. I don't know about you, but I'm dying to see what GPT's response is to this prompt.

GPT response: *1. "Co-authored with AI: A Human-ChatGPT Collaboration"*

2. "AI-Enhanced Creativity: Human and ChatGPT Unite"

3. "A Symbiotic Symphony: The Harmony of Human and ChatGPT Minds"

4. "The Art of AI Fusion: Blending Human Ingenuity with ChatGPT's Capabilities"

5. "Cerebral Convergence: Human Expertise Meets ChatGPT's Computational Power"

6. "Intelligent Interplay: A Creative Dance Between Human and ChatGPT"

7. "AI-Assisted Imagination: A Partnership Between Man and Machine"

8. "The Mind Meld: Merging Human Insight with ChatGPT's Proficiency"

9. "Forging the Future: A Human-AI Alliance in Education"

10. "The Creative Co-pilot: Soaring to New Heights with ChatGPT Collaboration"

Each of these descriptions highlights the unique relationship between human authorship and AI assistance, emphasizing the dynamic collaboration that results from combining human creativity with the powerful capabilities of ChatGPT. Choose the one that resonates the most with the overall theme and message of your book to give your readers an intriguing glimpse into the AI-human collaboration behind its creation.

Meh, not quite what I was looking for, but numbers 1 and 10 are close. I can keep clarifying my expectations and reiterating until I land on something that works. Hopefully by the time I finish this book, you'll see where I ended up on this, with it prominently displayed on the cover. Because in the spirit of AI ethics transparency, I think it's important to explain how I was able to whip these books out in a matter of weeks, and I'll probably be writing an AI-assisted collaboration about just that soon, but let's cover the basics. Let's turn once again to my collaborative partner for their input with this prompt, "please describe the iterative process I have used in collaboration with ChatGPT in the creation of this book."

GPT's response:

In the creation of this book, you have engaged in an iterative process of collaboration with ChatGPT, leveraging the strengths of both human and AI to enhance the final product. This process involved several stages, as outlined below:

1. Idea Generation: You initiated the process by providing ChatGPT with prompts, questions, or topics relevant to your book. ChatGPT responded with ideas, examples, and suggestions to help you expand upon and refine your initial concepts.

2. Drafting and Refinement: You used ChatGPT's input to create initial drafts of sections or chapters. During this phase, you continued to interact with ChatGPT, asking for clarifications, revisions, or alternative suggestions to improve the content. You integrated ChatGPT's responses with your own ideas and expertise to shape the narrative.

3. Review and Feedback: As you completed drafts, you periodically revisited the content with ChatGPT to assess its quality, coherence, and relevance. You asked ChatGPT for feedback, which led to further revisions and refinements. This iterative process of review and feedback enabled you to polish the content and ensure it met your desired standards.

4. Structuring and Organization: In collaboration with ChatGPT, you determined the best way to structure and organize your book. This included deciding on the order of chapters, sections, or topics, as well as creating smooth transitions and connections between different parts of the book.

5. Fine-Tuning and Finalization: Once the content was in place, you continued your collaboration with ChatGPT to fine-tune the language, style, and tone of the book. This involved making adjustments to ensure consistency, clarity, and readability, while also addressing any remaining concerns or gaps in the content.

Throughout this process, you maintained a dynamic and flexible relationship with ChatGPT, treating it as a creative partner and valuable resource. By combining your human expertise with ChatGPT's AI capabilities, you were able to achieve a level of insight, creativity, and nuance that would have been challenging to attain alone. This iterative process of collaboration has resulted in a unique, engaging, and informative book that showcases the potential of AI-human partnerships in the realm of writing and education.

As you can see, one can't simply say, "write a book on using chat-GPT for teachers." Well, I suppose you could, but it would likely be crap, and if you weren't there to give your own anecdotes, perspective, experience, opinions, and insight, the book may be nothing more than a heartless manual with unchecked sources, a lack of connection and relevance to the human aspects of your topic. As an audiobook narrator, I have definitely come across books that were generated by AI without much human input, and just as we teachers have a special eye for spotting something that wasn't written by our students, it was pretty evident that these types of books were direct copy and paste from GPT. While you can certainly generate content that way, I, for one, would not feel comfortable or proud putting my own name on as the "author" of such content.

And with that, the ethics debate in AI is just getting started, so be part of the conversation and encourage your students to do the same. Walk through exercises like the one in this chapter with them and see where their ethical rabbit hole leads.

Reflections on AI Ethics

As the sun dipped below the horizon, casting a warm glow across the classroom, Ms. Key leaned back in her chair, her mind filled with thoughts on the ethical uses and responsibilities of AI in education. She had spent the day sharing her newfound knowledge and experiences with her students, emphasizing the importance of responsible AI usage, and she was proud of the discussions and insights they had generated together.

Ms. Key recalled how her students had eagerly engaged in a lively debate about the implications of AI-generated content, pondering the difference between collaboration and outright plagiarism. The students had raised thought-provoking questions and offered unique perspectives, which only fueled Ms. Key's passion for exploring this new technological frontier.

She knew that as a teacher, she had a responsibility to not only educate her students about AI but to model ethical behavior in her own interactions with the technology. By using AI as a tool to enhance her teaching, rather than relying on it as a crutch or replacement, she demonstrated to her students the value of combining human expertise with AI capabilities.

Ms. Key reflected on the importance of fostering critical thinking skills in her students, enabling them to discern the validity and relevance of AI-generated content. By encouraging them to question and challenge the output of AI tools, she was equipping them with the necessary skills to navigate an increasingly technology-driven world.

As she glanced around the classroom, Ms. Key couldn't help but feel a sense of pride in her students' growing understanding of digital citizenship. They had embraced the need to use AI ethically, recognizing the importance of respecting others' intellectual property and being mindful of their digital footprint. She knew that cultivating these values would set her students up for success in the future.

Looking ahead, Ms. Key realized that her journey with AI was far from over. As technology continued to evolve, she was committed to staying informed and adapting her teaching methods to best serve her students. By embracing AI as a creative partner and teaching her students to use it responsibly and ethically, she was confident that they would be well-prepared to face the challenges and opportunities that lay ahead.

With a contented sigh, Ms. Key gathered her belongings and switched off the classroom lights, excited to continue exploring the world of AI with her students. As she stepped out into the cool evening air, she knew that together, they were charting a course for a brighter, more ethical, and innovative future in education.

Chapter 5

Embracing AI as a Creative Partner

Ms. Key was initially skeptical about the idea of integrating AI into her teaching practices. She saw AI as a potential threat to student learning and a source of plagiarism. However, with an open mind and a determination to explore the capabilities and possibilities of AI, Ms. Key embarked on a transformative journey that led her to view AI as an invaluable creative partner.

In this chapter, we will follow Ms. Key's journey as she discovers the many ways AI can collaborate with educators and students to enhance creativity, critical thinking, and problem-solving. Together, we'll explore the endless possibilities that emerge when AI technology is seamlessly integrated into the classroom.

Our first stop on this journey will be the realm of AI-powered brainstorming and idea generation. Witness how Ms. Key learns to harness the power of AI to spark inspiration and ignite her students' creativity, breaking through barriers and generating a plethora of ideas for tackling projects and assignments.

Next, join Ms. Key as she delves into the world of collaborative writing and editing with AI. Watch as she learns to effectively combine her human touch with the analytical abilities of AI, resulting in engaging and captivating writing. Along the way, she'll discover how AI can assist in editing and refining her students' work, turning rough drafts into polished, well-crafted pieces.

As we continue, we'll accompany Ms. Key as she examines the ways AI can enhance multimedia projects. From video editing and animation to music composition, observe how she uncovers various methods for AI to elevate her students' work, enabling them to create impressive and immersive multimedia presentations.

Our journey will then lead us to explore how Ms. Key focuses on building her students' creativity and critical thinking skills. We'll delve into the strategies she employs to nurture a love of exploration, questioning, and innovation, using AI as a valuable tool to support her students' growth. By fostering their curiosity and resourcefulness, Ms. Key sets them on a path to a lifetime of confident, creative thinking.

Finally, we'll share real-life case studies of successful AI-human collaboration, inspired by Ms. Key's experiences and those of other educators. Through these stories of teachers and students working together with AI to achieve exceptional creative and learning outcomes, we'll provide inspiration and valuable insights into the potential of AI as a creative partner.

So, come along with Ms. Key on this exciting journey through the fascinating world of AI as a Creative Partner. Together, we'll uncover tools, techniques, and strategies that will help us navigate this new landscape, empowering ourselves and our students to embrace the true potential of human ingenuity when combined with AI technology.

Prompting Creativity

It's a cozy, rainy afternoon, and Ms. Key is gathered with her students, eager to embark on a new project. But alas, the wellspring of ideas seems to have dried up, and the creative juices just aren't flowing. Fear not, for the magical world of AI-powered brainstorming and idea generation is here to save the day!

One of my favorite tools in the morning to help organize my thoughts so I can tackle my day is AudioPen.ai which is an AI-powered tool that allows you to speak up to 15 minutes, then transcribes it and summarizes it. At the time of this writing in April 2023, the paid version limit is 15 minutes, however the creator of this tool is making updates and improvements daily, so it's possible that by the time this book finds itself in your hands, on your screen, or in your ears, that may have changed. As one of the early users, I've been able to follow the creator's constant iterations, which is just another fascinating part of this AI journey. I love AudioPen not just because it helps organize my racing ADHD thoughts, but because it gives me a reason to walk for 15 minutes. I grab the dogs and my phone, and off we go, exercising our bodies and minds.

With AI technology like GPT and tools like AudioPen by our side, we can conjure up a storm of ideas, perfect for those moments when inspiration seems to be playing hide-and-seek. So let's dive into some practical and applicable examples that'll get our creative engines revving, with AI as our trusty co-pilot.

1. The Idea Blender:

Have your students create a list of random words or concepts, and then use GPT to generate ideas that combine these elements in unexpected and delightful ways. For example, if they provide the words "ocean," "solar power," and "roller coaster," GPT might suggest an eco-friendly, solar-powered roller coaster that travels across the ocean floor, teaching riders about marine conservation.

Prompt ideas:

a. "Create a new animal species that combines the features of a giraffe, a dolphin, and a hedgehog. Describe its habitat, diet, and unique abilities."

b. "Invent a futuristic mode of transportation that uses elements from nature, such as wind or plant growth, as its primary power source."

c. "Generate a concept for a unique sport or game that incorporates elements from basketball, archery, and ice skating."

2. Story Starters:

Using GPT, generate a series of unique story prompts to kickstart your students' creative writing. For instance, GPT might come up with a scenario like, "In a world where people communicate only through interpretive dance, a young girl discovers she has the power to control the weather with her movements." Have your students use these prompts as jumping-off points for their own stories, poems, or plays.

Prompt ideas:

a. "Write a story about a world where people can only see one color each, and the protagonist discovers a way to share their unique color with others."

b. "Create a story set in a society where people gain superpowers based on their favorite food."

c. "Compose a tale about a time-traveling historian who accidentally changes the course of history and must fix their mistake."

3. Debate Topics:

Generate a list of thought-provoking and unusual debate topics using GPT, and then have your students research and discuss their positions. For example, GPT might propose, "Should humans be allowed to colonize other planets if it means displacing or harming alien species?" or "If we could eradicate all mosquitoes, should we?"

Prompt ideas:

a. "Should we establish a global government to address the world's most pressing issues, such as climate change and poverty?"
b. "Is it ethical to use AI and advanced technology to create realistic simulations of deceased loved ones?"
c. "Should there be a limit to how much personal data companies can collect and use for targeted advertising?"

4. Art Mashups:

Using GPT, combine famous artworks or art movements to inspire your students' original creations. GPT could suggest ideas like, "Imagine if Vincent van Gogh had painted 'Starry Night' using the bright colors and geometric shapes of the Cubist movement" or "What if Leonardo da Vinci's 'The Last Supper' featured characters from classic fairy tales instead of Jesus and his disciples?" Encourage your students to interpret these mashups in their own unique ways, through painting, sculpture, or digital art. You can also use tools like Midjourney, DALL*E or apps like AI Arta to generate images based on prompts, such as the cover art on this book, which was created using AI Arta app with the prompt "happy curly haired teacher with a tiny robot in a cheerful classroom." Be sure to follow your favorite tech gurus on Twitter or other social media for the latest and greatest tools like these.

Prompt ideas:

a. "Imagine if Salvador Dali had created a surrealist interpretation of Michelangelo's 'The Creation of Adam.' What elements would be present?"
b. "Create an artwork that combines elements of Pop Art with the intricate patterns of Islamic art."

c. "Design a sculpture inspired by both the fluidity of Art Nouveau and the rigid geometry of Brutalist architecture."

5. Future Predictions:

Prompt GPT to generate predictions for how various aspects of society might change in the future, and then have your students research and debate the plausibility of these ideas. For instance, GPT might suggest that, "In the year 2100, people will live in underwater cities powered by giant kelp forests" or "By 2050, all cars will be replaced by teleportation devices." How realistic are these visions? What are the potential benefits and drawbacks? As you can start to see, the more creative you can get with prompts, the more fun you can have!

More prompt ideas:

a. "What changes might we see in education by the year 2050, with the increasing integration of AI and virtual reality technology?"
b. "How could our understanding and treatment of mental health evolve over the next century?"
c. "What new forms of entertainment and leisure activities might emerge as technology advances and our society changes?"

6. Math Puzzles:

Using GPT, create fun and challenging math puzzles for your students to solve. For example, GPT could generate a riddle like, "Three friends go to a restaurant and order a pizza. Each person eats exactly one-third of the pizza, but they all eat a different number of slices. How is this possible?" (Hint: The pizza is cut into different-sized slices!)

More prompt ideas:

a. "Create a logic puzzle involving the seating arrangement of guests at a dinner party, based on specific criteria (e.g., A can't sit next to B, C must sit across from D)."
b. "Generate a unique math riddle that involves the use of prime

numbers and divisibility rules."

c. "Design a geometry challenge that asks students to calculate the area of an irregular shape using their knowledge of triangles and polygons."

7. Science Experiments:

Ask GPT to suggest innovative science experiments for your students to conduct. GPT might propose ideas like, "Create a homemade water filter using materials found in nature, and test its effectiveness at removing pollutants" or "Build a miniature greenhouse and investigate how different colored lights affect plant growth." Encourage students to brainstorm as many "What would happen if..." questions as they can and groups can share out their questions and GPT's answers.

More prompt ideas:

a. "Suggest an experiment that investigates the effects of different music genres on plant growth."

b. "Create a hands-on activity for students to explore the principles of magnetism using everyday materials."

c. "Design an experiment to test the efficiency of various homemade solar cookers."

8. History What-Ifs:

Use GPT to generate "what-if" scenarios for historical events, and have your students research and discuss the potential outcomes. For example, GPT might pose questions like, "What if the ancient Egyptians had discovered electricity?" or "How might history have unfolded if the Library of Alexandria had never been destroyed?" Encourage your students to use their critical thinking skills and historical knowledge to explore these alternative timelines.

More prompt ideas:

a. "What might have happened if the printing press had been invented during the time of ancient Rome?"

b. "Explore the potential consequences if the United States had not entered World War II."

c. "How would the world be different if the Industrial Revolution had begun in Asia instead of Europe?"

9. Design Challenges:

Prompt GPT to come up with unique design challenges for your students to tackle. For instance, GPT might suggest, "Design a treehouse that can adapt to different environments and climates" or "Create a wearable technology that helps people stay connected to nature." Have your students work in teams to brainstorm, sketch, and present their innovative solutions.

More prompt ideas:

a. "Create a prototype for an eco-friendly, multi-functional piece of furniture for small living spaces."

b. "Design a public park that caters to the needs of both humans and local wildlife, promoting coexistence and sustainability."

c. "Invent a wearable device that helps individuals with sensory processing disorders navigate and cope with their environment."

10. Musical Mashups:

Using GPT, generate unexpected combinations of musical styles, instruments, or themes for your students to explore in their compositions. For example, GPT might propose, "Compose a piece that combines the sounds of a symphony orchestra with traditional Japanese instruments, inspired by the life cycle of a butterfly" or "Create a rap song that tells the story of an epic journey through outer space." Encourage your students to think outside the box and push the boundaries of their musical creativity.

More prompt ideas:

a. "Compose a piece of music that combines elements of classical music with electronic dance music (EDM)."

b. "Create a mashup of traditional folk music from different cultures, showcasing the similarities and differences in rhythms, melodies, and instruments."

c. "Develop a musical performance that combines elements of jazz and choral singing, exploring the interplay between improvisation and harmony."

With these practical and applicable examples, you'll have no shortage of ways to spark your students' imaginations and ignite their creative fires, and when you run out of ideas, ask GPT for more! By incorporating AI-powered brainstorming and idea generation into your lessons, you're not only fostering a sense of wonder and exploration, but you're also teaching your students to harness the power of technology as a tool for creative expression and problem-solving. So go on, take a leap into the world of AI-fueled creativity, and watch as your classroom transforms into a veritable garden of ideas, ripe for the picking!

For those of you in an **independent study setting**, here are a few more ideas tailored to you and your students:

1. The AI Autobiography:

Encourage your independent study students to explore their own lives through the lens of AI by having them generate an AI-written autobiography. Have them provide GPT with a brief overview of their life story, including important events, accomplishments, and personal reflections. Then, ask them to refine and edit the AI-generated content, adding their own insights and emotions to create a unique and engaging narrative. This activity will help students gain a deeper understanding of their own lives while developing their creative writing and editing skills.

2. The AI Debate:

Have your independent study students engage in an AI-assisted debate on a topic of their choice. Instruct them to use GPT to generate arguments for both sides of the issue, ensuring that they present well-rounded and balanced viewpoints. Then, have them evaluate the AI-generated arguments, identify logical fallacies or weaknesses, and strengthen their own understanding of the topic. This exercise will help students develop critical thinking, analytical, and persuasive skills, all while fostering a responsible and ethical use of AI.

3. The AI Research Assistant:

Encourage your independent study students to utilize GPT as a research assistant for a project or paper. Have them input their research questions or topics into GPT and analyze the generated content for useful information, sources, and ideas. Instruct them to critically evaluate the accuracy and relevance of the AI-generated content, using it as a starting point for further research and inquiry. This activity will help students become more discerning consumers of AI-generated content and develop essential research skills.

4. AI-Generated Poetry:

Challenge your independent study students to create a collection of AI-generated poetry based on a theme or style of their choice. Have them input relevant prompts or keywords into GPT, then work with the AI-generated content to refine and shape the poems. Encourage them to experiment with different poetic forms, structures, and techniques to create a diverse and engaging collection. This activity will help students develop their creative writing and editing skills while exploring the potential of AI as a creative partner in the arts.

5. The AI Study Buddy:

Invite your independent study students to use GPT as a study buddy for reviewing and consolidating their learning. Have them input questions, problems, or topics from their course materials into GPT, then analyze the AI-generated content for accuracy, clarity, and usefulness. Encourage them to use the AI-generated content as a starting point for discussion, reflection, and further learning, actively engaging with the material to reinforce their understanding. This activity will help students take ownership of their learning while demonstrating the potential of AI as a supportive and collaborative learning tool.

AI-Enhanced Multimedia Projects

As we've ventured deeper into the digital age, multimedia projects have become a staple in education, allowing students to express their creativity and showcase their understanding through various forms of media. In this ever-evolving landscape, AI and GPT can be powerful allies, helping students and educators alike to elevate their multimedia projects and bring their ideas to life. Let's dive into the wonderful world of AI-enhanced multimedia projects, exploring practical examples that you can implement in your classroom right away.

1. AI-Powered Visual Storytelling:

Visual storytelling is a captivating way for students to communicate their ideas, and AI can be an invaluable assistant in this process. Encourage students to create digital comics, storyboards, or graphic novels by using GPT to generate dialogue, captions, and even plot ideas. Students can then use their artistic skills or online illustration tools to bring the AI-generated content to life, creating a compelling and engaging narrative. This activity not only fosters creativity but also helps students develop essential skills in visual communication and storytelling.

2. AI-Generated Voice Overs and Podcasts:

The realm of audio content is booming, and AI can help students create compelling voice overs or podcasts for their multimedia projects. Have students use GPT to generate scripts, interviews, or monologues on a chosen topic. Then, using text-to-speech software or their own voice, they can transform the AI-generated text into an audio recording. This activity will help students develop essential skills in scriptwriting, storytelling, and audio production, while also showcasing the creative potential of AI.

3. AI-Enhanced Video Projects:

Video projects can be a powerful medium for students to express their ideas, and AI can help them elevate their work to new heights. Have students use GPT to generate story ideas, scripts, or even shot lists for their video projects. They can then use their creativity, filmmaking skills, and available resources to bring the AI-generated content to life on screen. This activity will help students develop essential skills in video production, storytelling, and collaboration, while also demonstrating the creative capabilities of AI.

4. AI-Inspired Music and Soundtracks:

Music and sound play an integral role in multimedia projects, and AI can help students create original and engaging soundscapes. Have students use GPT to generate lyrics, melodies, or even entire compositions based on a theme or emotion. They can then use digital music production tools or traditional instruments to bring the AI-generated content to life, creating a unique soundtrack for their projects. This activity will help students develop their musical skills and creative expression while exploring the potential of AI in the world of music.

5. AI-Driven Interactive Experiences:

Interactive experiences, such as games, simulations, or virtual reality, can provide students with immersive and engaging ways to explore concepts and ideas. With the help of GPT, students can generate game scenarios, puzzles, or interactive storylines that can be brought to life using coding skills or online game development tools. This activity will help students develop essential skills in problem-solving, design, and programming while showcasing the creative potential of AI in interactive media.

6. AI-Assisted Data Visualization and Infographics:

Data visualization and infographics are powerful tools for communicating complex information in a clear and engaging manner. Have students use GPT to generate ideas, facts, or statistics related to a specific topic or research question. They can then use data visualization tools or graphic design software to create visually appealing and informative infographics or data visualizations based on the AI-generated content. This activity will help students develop essential skills in research, data analysis, and visual communication while showcasing the potential of AI as a research assistant.

As you can see, the possibilities for AI-enhanced multimedia projects are vast and varied, limited only by your imagination and the creativity of your students. By incorporating GPT and AI into your classroom, you can help students unlock new levels of creativity, critical thinking, and innovation. The examples provided above serve as a starting point to inspire you and your students to explore the boundless potential of AI in multimedia projects.

It's essential to keep the conversation around ethical AI use open and ongoing, ensuring that students understand the power and responsibility that comes with these tools. By fostering a culture of honesty, transparency, and ethical AI use, you'll be preparing your students to harness this technology in ways that are both responsible and transformative.

Ultimately, the goal is to empower students to use AI and GPT as creative partners, working together to generate ideas and content that push the boundaries of what's possible in education. By embracing the potential of AI-powered multimedia projects, you'll be giving your students the opportunity to develop essential 21st-century skills while also fostering a culture of creativity, innovation, and responsible technology use in your classroom.

So, as you embark on this exciting journey with your students, remember to keep an open mind, embrace the potential of AI, and explore the many ways in which GPT can enrich your multimedia projects. By doing so, you'll be nurturing a generation of creative thinkers, problem solvers, and responsible technology users, all while providing them with the tools they need to thrive in a rapidly changing world.

Building Student Creativity and Critical Thinking

Imagine your students chatting excitedly in the classroom, their eyes lit up with the spark of inspiration, and their fingertips flying across their devices as they work with their new creative partner, GPT. This could be your classroom, a haven for cultivating creativity and critical thinking among your students. How, you ask? Well, buckle up, because we're about to dive into a world of imaginative possibilities!

First, let's tackle creative writing. You know the drill: students staring at blank pages, the pesky writer's block rearing its ugly head. Enter GPT, the ultimate brainstorming buddy! Give students a topic or a prompt, and let them work with GPT to generate unique story ideas, character descriptions, or even entire passages. Here's a fun example to get those creative juices flowing: students could use GPT to create a fantastical world inhabited by magical creatures. They could ask GPT questions about this world, such as "What do the houses look like?" or "What's the most popular sport?" The sky's the limit, and students will be delighted by the intriguing responses GPT provides.

Speaking of collaboration, why not let students team up with GPT for group projects? Students could be assigned roles in the group, and

GPT could act as an additional member, offering fresh perspectives, ideas, or solutions to problems the group is tackling. This kind of collaboration not only sparks creativity but also fosters critical thinking as students learn to evaluate the AI-generated input and decide which ideas to incorporate into their project.

Now, let's talk about those pesky debates and discussions. You know, the ones where students are hesitant to share their opinions, unsure of their reasoning or just feeling a little shy. With GPT on their side, students can develop well-rounded arguments by using the AI to generate pros and cons for a given topic. This way, students can explore different perspectives, refine their reasoning, and gain the confidence to voice their opinions in class. Plus, it's a great opportunity for some lively, thought-provoking discussions!

But wait, there's more! Have you ever considered using GPT to create interactive, choose-your-own-adventure stories? This is a fantastic way to engage students in narrative development and decision-making. Students can start by writing a story introduction and then offer several choices for the reader to make. They can use GPT to generate possible outcomes for each choice, then continue the process until they've crafted a multi-layered, interactive story. This activity not only encourages creativity but also hones critical thinking skills as students consider the consequences of each choice and devise compelling storylines.

And finally, let's not forget the power of reflection. Encourage students to use GPT to write journal entries or self-assessments about their learning experiences, challenges, and successes. By prompting GPT with questions or statements about their thoughts, students can gain insights and suggestions for improvement. This reflective practice fosters self-awareness, metacognition, and critical thinking as students evaluate their learning process and set goals for future growth.

So, there you have it, a treasure trove of ideas to help you and your students harness the magic of GPT for cultivating creativity and critical thinking. Remember, these examples are just the tip of the iceberg—feel free to put on your rose-colored glasses and explore the infinite potential GPT has to offer. By doing so, you'll be nurturing a generation of imaginative, analytical thinkers who are ready to take on the world, one creative endeavor at a time. Happy exploring, fellow educators!

Successful Uses of AI and GPT in the Classroom: A New Approach to Teaching

The advent of artificial intelligence (AI) and GPT technologies, such as ChatGPT, has opened up a world of possibilities for educators. By leveraging these cutting-edge tools, teachers can make learning more interactive, personalized, and engaging. Here are some successful uses of AI and GPT in the classroom:

1. Interactive Grammar Lessons:

Teachers can use ChatGPT to create dynamic, collaborative activities for grammar lessons. Students can work together to edit a piece of writing with grammatical errors and then compare their edits to those made by ChatGPT. This approach encourages students to critically evaluate the AI's performance while reinforcing their understanding of grammatical rules.

Sample prompts:

a. "Generate a short paragraph with five grammatical errors for students to identify and correct."
b. "Create a dialogue between two characters with errors in verb tense consistency."

c. "Provide a list of ten sentences, half of which contain subject-verb agreement mistakes."

d. "Generate a paragraph that demonstrates the incorrect use of homophones."

e. "Compose a text with several misplaced or dangling modifiers for students to correct."

2. Customized Study Guides:

AI and GPT technologies can help educators design tailored study guides for each student. By inputting a student's work, ChatGPT can generate a customized guide that highlights areas for improvement and provides relevant resources. This approach saves time for teachers while ensuring that assessments and feedback cater to individual students' needs.

Sample prompts:

a. "Based on this student's essay, suggest three areas for improvement and relevant resources to help them."

b. "Create a personalized study guide on fractions for a student struggling with this concept."

c. "Generate a list of vocabulary words and definitions tailored to a student's reading level."

d. "Design a customized learning plan for a student who needs extra help with writing skills."

e. "Based on this student's math test results, provide a study plan targeting their weak areas."

3. Flipped Classroom:

With AI and GPT tools, teachers can implement a flipped classroom model where students learn new material independently and then participate in interactive activities during class time. By using ChatGPT to gather information on a specific topic, students can spend more time analyzing and engaging with the content, leading to deeper understanding and improved higher-order thinking skills.

Sample prompts:

a. "Generate a concise summary of the key concepts in photosynthesis for students to study before class."

b. "Create a list of engaging discussion questions for a flipped classroom session on the American Revolution."

c. "Provide a step-by-step guide for students to independently learn about the water cycle."

d. "Generate an interactive quiz on the basics of economics for students to complete before class."

e. "Design a pre-class assignment for students to research the causes and effects of climate change."

4. Developing Information Literacy Skills:

AI and GPT technologies can play a critical role in helping students build information literacy skills. Teachers can use ChatGPT to demonstrate the importance of evaluating the credibility and reliability of AI-generated information. By comparing ChatGPT's outputs with other online sources, students can learn to identify biases and inaccuracies in digital content.

Sample prompts:

a. "Generate a list of tips for evaluating the credibility of online sources."

b. "Create a fake news article with several factual inaccuracies for students to identify."

c. "Provide examples of biased language in a text and ask students to rewrite it objectively."

d. "Generate a list of commonly used logical fallacies and have students find examples online."

e. "Design an activity where students compare the reliability of different sources on the same topic."

5. Collaborative Writing Projects:

Using GPT technologies, teachers can encourage students to participate in group writing projects. ChatGPT can help generate ideas, provide suggestions for improvement, and even contribute to the story itself. This collaborative approach fosters creativity, teamwork, and communication among students.

Sample prompts:

a. "Generate a story prompt for a group writing project."

b. "Provide feedback on this group's collaborative story and suggest areas for improvement."

c. "Generate a list of interesting characters for a collaborative writing project."

d. "Create a series of plot twists for students to incorporate into their collaborative story."

e. "Suggest three possible endings for a group-written story and have students vote on their favorite."

6. Foreign Language Learning:

AI and GPT technologies can be used to support foreign language learning by providing instant feedback, translations, and explanations. Students can practice their language skills in real-time, while teachers can monitor their progress and identify areas that need improvement.

Sample prompts:

a. "Translate this English sentence into Spanish and provide a brief explanation of the grammar used."

b. "Generate a list of common French vocabulary words for beginners."

c. "Create a dialogue in German for intermediate students to practice their speaking skills."

d. "Provide a list of idiomatic expressions in Italian for students to learn and practice."

e. "Correct the errors in this Chinese text and explain the mistakes to the student."

7. Creative Problem Solving:

Teachers can use ChatGPT to generate thought-provoking questions and scenarios, challenging students to come up with innovative solutions. This approach helps develop critical thinking and problem-solving skills, preparing students for real-world challenges.

Sample prompts:

a. "Generate a real-world problem related to environmental conservation for students to solve."

b. "Create a hypothetical scenario in which students must develop a plan to manage limited resources."

c. "Design a challenge where students must come up with a marketing strategy for a new product."

d. "Pose a moral dilemma for students to debate and consider different perspectives."

e. "Generate a list of inventive prompts that encourage students to think outside the box."

Incorporating AI and GPT technologies like ChatGPT into the classroom can lead to more engaging, interactive, and personalized learning experiences. By embracing these tools, educators can make a positive impact on student outcomes and prepare them for a future where technology plays an increasingly important role.

Practical Applications to Maximize Teacher Efficiency (or, How to Finally Get Your Life Back)

This is the section that your family, friends, significant others, and dogs are going to appreciate just as much as you – how to use AI and GPT to help with those time-devouring tasks, freeing up your mind and time to do more of what you love inside and outside the classroom. Honestly, AI's ability to help me organize my thoughts, inbox, and life is what is allowing me to write this book while still teaching 40 hours a week, curriculum writing 10 hours a week, and playing with my dogs as much as humanly possible amid the other responsibilities. Let's take a look at our dear Ms. Key and how she is using AI and GPT tools to give her more time to focus on the aspects of her job that drew her there in the first place: connecting with and helping every student, collaborating with creative colleagues, and sharing her passion for her content area and her love of learning.

As the morning sun filters through the classroom window, Ms. Key sips her coffee and logs into her computer. Thanks to AI-powered tools like ChatGPT, she can now approach her day with confidence, knowing that her workload is more manageable than ever. She uses AI to create dynamic lesson plans, freeing her up to provide one-on-one support to her students. During her planning period, she collaborates with her peers on exciting new projects, and she even has time to work on the book she's always wanted to write.

Lesson Planning

ChatGPT Lesson Plan Generator: Ms. Key uses ChatGPT to generate a lesson plan tailored to her subject, grade level, and teaching style. This saves her countless hours spent researching and preparing

lesson plans, allowing her to focus on student engagement and interaction.

- Prompt 1: "Generate a lesson plan for a 6th-grade science class."

- Prompt 2: "Create a high school English lesson plan focused on poetry analysis."

- Prompt 3: "Design a college-level history lesson on the American Revolution."

Content Creation

AI-generated Study Guides: By inputting student work into Chat-
GPT, Ms. Key can generate customized study guides that highlight
areas for improvement and provide relevant resources. This saves her
time and ensures that assessments and feedback cater to individual
students' needs.

- Prompt 1: "Create a study guide for a student struggling with algebra."

- Prompt 2: "Generate a study guide for a student who needs help in world history."

- Prompt 3: "Design a study guide for improving essay writing skills."

Interactive Classroom Activities

Collaborative Writing Projects with ChatGPT: Ms. Key uses Chat-
GPT to help students generate ideas, provide suggestions for improvement, and contribute to group writing projects. This collaborative approach fosters creativity, teamwork, and communication
among students.

- Prompt 1: "Generate a story idea for a group of students to work on together."

- Prompt 2: "Provide feedback on a paragraph written by a student."

- Prompt 3: "Suggest ways to improve a student's persuasive essay."

Language Learning

AI-assisted Foreign Language Practice: By using AI and GPT tools, Ms. Key can provide instant feedback, translations, and explanations for students learning a foreign language. This helps students practice their language skills in real-time, while allowing her to monitor their progress and identify areas that need improvement.

- Prompt 1: "Translate this English sentence into Spanish."

- Prompt 2: "Explain the grammar rules behind this French sentence."

- Prompt 3: "Provide a pronunciation guide for this German word."

Problem Solving

Creative Problem Solving with ChatGPT: Ms. Key uses ChatGPT to generate thought-provoking questions and scenarios, challenging students to come up with innovative solutions. This approach helps develop critical thinking and problem-solving skills, preparing students for real-world challenges.

- Prompt 1: "Generate a critical thinking question for high school students."

- Prompt 2: "Create a real-world problem for students to solve using math skills."

- Prompt 3: "Design a scenario that requires creative problem solving."

Grading and Assessment

AI-powered Grading Assistance: By utilizing AI tools, Ms. Key can automate the grading process, saving time and providing consistent, unbiased evaluations. This allows her to focus on providing personalized feedback and support to her students.

- Prompt 1: "Grade this student's short answer response."

- Prompt 2: "Evaluate this essay and provide feedback on its strengths and weaknesses."

- Prompt 3: "Assess this student's performance on a math problem."

Classroom Management

ChatGPT for Classroom Policies and Procedures: Ms. Key uses ChatGPT to create and maintain classroom policies and procedures that are clear, fair, and consistent. By automating this process, she can spend more time addressing individual student needs and fostering a positive learning environment.

- Prompt 1: "Generate a series of fun activities to help a class create norms together."

- Prompt 2: "Create a set of procedures for group work in a middle school science class."

- Prompt 3: "Design a classroom management plan for an elementary school classroom."

Professional Development

AI-assisted Professional Learning: Ms. Key utilizes AI tools to personalize her professional development, accessing resources and learning opportunities tailored to her needs and interests. This allows her to grow as an educator and better serve her students.

- Prompt 1: "Recommend professional development resources for teaching online."

- Prompt 2: "Suggest strategies for promoting equity and inclusion in the classroom."

- Prompt 3: "Provide tips for effective classroom management."

Parent Communication

AI-enhanced Parent-Teacher Communication: By using AI and GPT tools, Ms. Key can streamline communication with parents, providing updates on student progress and addressing concerns more efficiently. This helps foster stronger relationships between home and school, ensuring a supportive learning environment for all students.

- Prompt 1: "Compose an email update for parents about their child's academic progress and step-by-step instructions for creating a mail merge."

- Prompt 2: "Generate a parent-teacher conference agenda that addresses a student's strengths and areas for growth."

- Prompt 3: "Create a newsletter for parents that highlights classroom achievements and upcoming events."

Curriculum Development

AI-powered Curriculum Design: Ms. Key uses AI tools to create engaging, differentiated, and standards-aligned curricula for her students. This saves her time and ensures that her instruction is tailored to the diverse needs of her learners.

- Prompt 1: "Design a standards-aligned math unit for 5th grade."

- Prompt 2: "Generate a project-based learning unit for a high school social studies class."

- Prompt 3: "Create an interdisciplinary unit that combines science and language arts for middle school students."

Ms. Key's day is filled with meaningful interactions and opportunities to support her students, thanks to the integration of AI and GPT technologies in her classroom. By embracing these powerful tools, she has not only transformed her teaching practice but has also found the time to pursue her passion for writing. She starts by writing some suggestions for her teacher buddies at the independent study school down the street.

Independent Study Support

AI-guided Independent Study: For educators working in independent study settings, AI and GPT tools can be invaluable for providing personalized learning experiences that cater to the unique needs and interests of each student. This allows teachers to efficiently manage a diverse group of learners while ensuring that each individual receives the necessary support and guidance to thrive.

- Prompt 1: "Develop a personalized learning plan for a student interested in environmental science."

- Prompt 2: "Create a self-paced project outline for a student exploring graphic design."

- Prompt 3: "Generate a list of resources and activities for a student developing mental math skills."

In an independent study setting, Ms. Key's friends can use AI and GPT tools to generate customized learning plans, track student progress, and provide timely feedback. By streamlining these processes, they can effectively support each student's learning journey while maintaining a manageable workload. The integration of AI and GPT technologies also enables her to introduce unique, real-world experiences and challenges that keep students engaged and motivated, fostering a love for lifelong learning.

As the sun began to set, casting warm golden hues through the window, a group of teachers gathered around Ms. Key's dining table, sipping glasses of Pinot Noir to unwind after a particularly hectic week. State testing, new student enrollments, and the looming specter of parent-teacher conferences had left them all feeling drained and desperate for some downtime.

"You know, I just don't trust those AI thingies," grumbled Ms. Anderson, the school's enthusiastic, albeit skeptical, history teacher. "It's like, one minute they're helping you, and the next, they're making stuff up. I had a kid turn in an assignment citing sources that don't even exist!"

Ms. Key chuckled as she took a long sip of her Pinot Grigio. "I used to feel the same way, but honestly, it's changed my whole perspective on teaching. It's like having a creative partner, always ready to help and support you."

The room fell silent, the remaining teachers exchanging curious glances, their interest piqued. Ms. Johnson, a dedicated math teacher who had recently admitted to feeling overwhelmed, leaned in closer. "Tell us more, then. How has this AI thing helped you?"

Ms. Key took a deep breath and another sip, her eyes sparkling with excitement as she began to share her experiences. "Well, for starters, ChatGPT has been a game-changer for me. I've been using it to generate engaging grammar lessons, customized study guides for my students, and even to help me flip my classroom. My students are more involved, and I can focus on supporting their individual needs."

The teachers listened intently, their initial resistance melting away as Ms. Key excitedly recounted her successes. "But what about creativity?" asked Ms. Martinez, the school's resident art teacher. "Surely, AI can't help with that, in fact, I heard that it does all the thinking for you and turns your brain to mush. I overheard some students this morning talking about an app that can create realistic looking artwork – how are my students supposed to express themselves if they aren't even creating anything?"

"You'd be surprised," Ms. Key replied with a knowing smile. "I've been using GPT prompts to inspire my students in so many ways. It's given them the freedom to explore new ideas and perspectives, and it's even helped me discover a new love for writing, and rather than spend my wine money on a cover artist for my new book, I described what I wanted to my AI Arta app, and it generated the image I'm using for my cover! You guys know I love art, but I have to label stick figure drawings so the kiddos get the gist. This has been a life-altering for me!"

Ms. Key continued, describing how she'd been using AI and GPT tools to encourage collaborative writing projects, teach foreign languages, and foster creative problem-solving skills among her students. She shared her journey of embracing technology, rather than fighting it, and the positive impact it had made in her classroom.

"I've even been using it to help me manage my time and stress," she added. "With GPT tools, I can automate tasks like grading and lesson planning, leaving me more time to focus on what really matters: my students and their learning. But it's also helped me get some semblance of a work-life balance back. You guys know how I struggle with remembering my own self-care sometimes, so I've had GPT help me establish a manageable meditation schedule with daily affirmations tailored to what I want to work on."

As the conversation and wine flowed, Ms. Key shared the various strategies and tools she'd incorporated into her teaching practice. She explained how she used AI to enhance communication and collaboration among her fellow educators, and even to support students in an independent study setting. With each example, she offered GPT prompts that could help the teachers explore these new tools for themselves.

The teachers, eyebrows raised, exchanged glances, their skepticism slowly giving way to curiosity. Ms. Anderson raised her glass in a toast. "Well, I guess it's worth a shot. If it can help me survive parent-teacher conferences, I'm willing to try anything!"

The room filled with laughter, and the teachers clinked their glasses together, toasting to the future of education and the promise of AI and GPT technologies. As the evening wore on, they found themselves dreaming of the possibilities that awaited them and their students. For the first time in a long while, they felt a sense of hope and excitement, fueled by the knowledge that they had a new creative partner in their corner, ready to help them navigate the ever-changing tides of the educational ebb and flow.

And who knows? With this newfound support and the creative spark ignited in her own life, Ms. Key might just find the time and inspiration to finally write that book she's been thinking about for so long, now that she had the cover art to inspire her.

As the evening wound down and the teachers began to Uber home, they each carried with them a renewed sense of purpose and a new-found appreciation for the potential of AI and GPT technologies in their classrooms. They felt empowered to embrace these tools as partners in their quest to educate and inspire their students, rather than view them as just another burden on their already overflowing plates.

For Ms. Key and her fellow educators, the journey of incorporating AI and GPT into their teaching practices had only just begun. They knew there would be challenges, setbacks, and moments of doubt along the way, but they also knew that they were not alone. They had each other – and their new creative partner – to support them every step of the way.

In the weeks and months that followed, the teachers began to witness firsthand the transformative power of AI and GPT in their classrooms. They saw their students engage more deeply with their lessons, collaborate more effectively with their peers, and take ownership of their learning in ways they never thought possible. And as the teachers continued to explore the many ways in which AI and GPT could help them save time, reduce stress, and unleash their own creativity, they discovered that they, too, were capable of growing and evolving in ways they never imagined.

The journey was not always easy, but it was one that brought them closer together as educators, united in their shared mission to make a difference in the lives of their students. And as they continued to learn, adapt, and grow, they came to understand that embracing AI and GPT as a creative partner was not just about staying ahead of the curve – it was about unlocking the full potential of their students and themselves.

So, to all the teachers out there who are surfing the waves of the educational ebb and flow, remember this: AI and GPT technologies have the power to change the way we teach and learn, but only if we are willing to embrace them with open minds and open hearts. It's not about adding more to our plates; it's about finding new ways to support our students, our colleagues, and ourselves as we navigate the exciting and sometimes daunting world of education.

In the end, the true power of AI and GPT lies not in the technology itself, but in the creative and dedicated educators who use it to inspire, uplift, and empower their students to reach for the stars.

Ms. Key's Takeaways for AI as a Creative Partner:

Key Takeaway 1: AI tools can be a source of inspiration and support for students' creative processes.

GPT Prompts:

a. How can educators integrate AI tools into their lessons to inspire students' creativity and imagination?

b. What are some examples of AI tools that can help students explore new ideas and perspectives in their work?

c. How can teachers encourage students to use AI tools to expand their creative thinking and problem-solving skills?

d. In what ways can AI tools help students overcome creative blocks and foster original thinking?

e. How can educators ensure that AI tools are used as a complement to, rather than a replacement for, students' creativity?

Key Takeaway 2: Collaboration between students and AI tools can lead to innovative and unexpected outcomes.

GPT Prompts:

a. What are some examples of successful student-AI collaborations in creative projects?

b. How can teachers facilitate meaningful interactions between students and AI tools to enhance the creative process?

c. In what ways can AI tools challenge students' assumptions and help them think beyond traditional boundaries?

d. How can educators support students in leveraging AI tools to push the limits of their creative potential?

e. What are some strategies for fostering a sense of curiosity and exploration in student-AI collaborations?

Key Takeaway 3: Ethical considerations are crucial when using AI tools in creative projects.

GPT Prompts:

a. What are the ethical implications of using AI tools in creative projects, and how can educators address these concerns?

b. How can teachers help students understand the importance of giving proper credit and acknowledging AI's role in their creative work?

c. What are some strategies for ensuring that AI tools are used responsibly and ethically in the creative process?

d. How can educators encourage students to reflect on the potential consequences of their AI-generated creations?

e. What are some ways to teach students about the ethical considerations of AI-assisted authorship and intellectual property rights?

Key Takeaway 4: Developing a critical perspective on AI-generated content.

GPT Prompts:

a. How can educators teach students to evaluate the quality and relevance of AI-generated content in their creative work?

b. What are some strategies for helping students understand the limitations and biases of AI tools in the creative process?

c. How can teachers encourage students to question the assumptions and algorithms behind AI-generated content?

d. In what ways can educators promote a critical understanding of AI's role in shaping creative output?

e. How can teachers help students develop the skills to thoughtfully integrate AI-generated content into their creative work?

Key Takeaway 5: Encouraging student-led AI projects with creative and ethical considerations.

GPT Prompts:

a. What are some examples of student-led AI projects that incorporate both creative and ethical considerations?

b. How can educators support students in developing and executing AI projects that address real-world challenges and inspire creative solutions?

c. What are some strategies for fostering a culture of innovation and ethical responsibility in student-led AI projects?

d. How can teachers guide students in selecting and using AI tools that align with their creative goals and ethical values?

e. What are some ways educators can provide feedback and guidance on student-led AI projects while encouraging autonomy and ownership?

Chapter 6

Pushing the Boundaries of Creativity

How to Inspire GPT to Go Above and Beyond

F eeling the electric energy that comes from the powerful synergy between herself, her colleagues, and her students, Ms. Key decided to take her newfound passion for AI and education beyond the classroom. Over her summer break, she not only planned to write her book but also to craft a TED Talk that would resonate with educators around the world. She would share her journey of embracing AI in education and how it reignited her passion for teaching.

As she began to prepare her TED Talk, tentatively titled, "The AI Spark: Reigniting Your Passion for Education," Ms. Key turned to her trusted creative partner, GPT, for assistance. Together, they brainstormed the most engaging and inspiring content, drawing on her experiences and examples from her classroom and colleagues. GPT helped her refine her ideas and create a narrative that flowed seamlessly from start to finish, pulling the audience into her world and leaving them feeling inspired and motivated.

Continuing to work on her TED Talk, Ms. Key also began exploring ideas for a TED-Ed lesson for kids. She wanted to address the ethical use of AI, as well as provide fun and engaging ways for students to use it in their learning journey. With GPT by her side, she crafted a captivating lesson that not only educated children about the responsible use of AI but also demonstrated its potential to spark their curiosity and fuel their creativity.

As Ms. Key embarked on her journey, she discovered that the possibilities were endless. With GPT as her creative partner, she could bring her ideas to life in ways she never imagined possible. She could not only transform her own teaching practice but also inspire other educators and students to embrace the limitless potential of AI in education.

Together, Ms. Key and GPT were breaking down barriers and redefining the boundaries of creativity in the world of education. They were proving that by embracing AI and GPT technologies, teachers could not only reignite their passion for education but also create a more dynamic, engaging, and inspiring learning environment for their students.

So join us as we continue to push the boundaries of creativity and explore the transformative power of AI in education. Follow Ms. Key's journey as she takes the stage to share her experiences and insights in her TED Talk, and then dive into the world of ethical AI use and engaging learning activities with her TED-Ed lesson for kids. Together, let's embrace the power of AI and GPT to spark a new era of creativity, passion, and innovation in the world of education.

Pushing the Boundaries of Creativity: How to Inspire GPT to Go Above and Beyond

As Ms. Key embarked on her journey to create her TED Talk and TED-Ed lesson, she relied on these strategies to harness GPT's creative potential. Throughout her preparation process, she experimented with the following ultra-creative prompt concepts:

1. Be Specific with Your Prompts:

Clearly define your expectations by providing GPT with detailed prompts. The more specific your instructions, the better GPT can understand your vision and generate content aligned with your creative goals.

- "Create an engaging introduction for a TED Talk on AI in education that begins with an anecdote about a student's breakthrough moment."

- "Describe a fictional scenario in which AI has revolutionized the way we learn, highlighting the benefits and challenges of this new educational landscape."

- "Craft a compelling closing statement for a TED-Ed lesson that encourages students to consider the ethical implications of AI technology."

2. Encourage Divergent Thinking:

To foster out-of-the-box ideas, ask GPT to generate multiple concepts or perspectives on a topic. This approach encourages divergent thinking, allowing you to explore a broader range of creative possibilities.

- "Generate three distinct concepts for a TED-Ed lesson on ethical AI use, each targeting a different age group."

- "Provide five different perspectives on the role of AI in fostering creativity in the classroom."

- "Suggest three unique applications of AI technology that can address challenges faced by educators."

3. Set Constraints:

Sometimes, limitations can spark creativity. Set specific constraints for GPT, such as a unique writing style, a narrow theme, or unusual characters. These restrictions can lead to unexpected, inventive results.

- "Write a short story about the future of AI in education, using only words with four or fewer letters."

- "Describe a classroom setting where AI plays a central role, but the technology must be inspired by nature."

- "Create a dialogue between a teacher and an AI assistant where they communicate using only questions."

4. Combine Unrelated Ideas:

To inspire fresh perspectives, ask GPT to merge seemingly unrelated concepts or themes. This approach can lead to novel ideas and thought-provoking connections.

- "Imagine a world where AI-powered robots teach dance classes, exploring the intersection of technology, movement, and self-expression."

- "Describe an AI system that uses culinary arts to teach complex scientific concepts."

- "Develop a lesson plan that combines AI, historical events, and fashion design to explore cultural trends and their impact on society."

5. Iterate and Experiment:

Don't hesitate to iterate and refine your requests. As you experiment with different prompts and approaches, GPT's responses will evolve, potentially uncovering new creative avenues to explore.

- "Refine the following prompt to generate more imaginative ideas: 'Suggest ways AI can be used in a high school art class.'"

- "Experiment with different phrasings for a prompt about AI's role in supporting students with special needs."

- "Revise the following request to elicit more creative responses: 'Generate ideas for integrating AI into a literature lesson.'"

6. Leverage Randomness:

Introduce an element of randomness to your prompts, such as a surprise event or an unexpected character trait. This unpredictability can stimulate GPT's creative juices and yield intriguing outcomes.

- "Introduce a surprise twist in a story about an AI-powered tutoring system that leads to unexpected learning outcomes."

- "Describe a character with a unique trait who relies on AI to overcome personal challenges in an educational setting."

- "Imagine an AI system that unexpectedly develops a sense of humor, leading to unconventional teaching methods."

7. Build on GPT's Output:

Once GPT generates content, use it as a foundation to further your creative vision. By building on GPT's output, you can guide the AI in the desired direction, encouraging it to generate even more imaginative ideas.

- "Expand upon the following GPT-generated concept: 'An AI-powered virtual reality field trip to explore ancient civilizations.'"

- "Develop a lesson plan based on GPT's idea of using AI to create personalized learning paths for students."

- "Create a storyboard for a short film inspired by GPT's suggestion of an AI-assisted music composition class."

8. Seek Inspiration from Other Domains:

Encourage GPT to draw inspiration from various fields, like literature, art, history, or science. This interdisciplinary approach can inspire unique, thought-provoking creations that transcend traditional boundaries.

- "Design an AI-powered educational tool that incorporates principles from both neuroscience and gamification."

- "Imagine a teaching method that combines AI technology with insights from behavioral psychology to encourage positive learning habits."

- "Explore the intersection of AI, environmental science, and education to develop innovative ways to teach about climate change."

9. Challenge GPT's Assumptions:

Encourage GPT to question its own assumptions, biases, or preconceived notions. By pushing GPT to reevaluate its ideas, you can elicit more creative and unconventional responses.

- "Question the idea that AI will inevitably replace human teachers, and instead explore ways AI can complement and enhance human instruction."

- "Reevaluate the assumption that AI is inherently neutral, and consider how biases might emerge in AI-powered educational tools."

- "Challenge the notion that AI-driven personalization in education is universally beneficial, and discuss potential drawbacks and ethical concerns."

10. Foster Collaboration:

Collaborate with GPT in a back-and-forth conversation, allowing the AI to build upon your ideas and vice versa. This cooperative process can lead to a fruitful exchange of imaginative concepts and foster a synergy between human and AI creativity.

- "Engage in a back-and-forth conversation with GPT to brainstorm creative ways to teach a complex mathematical concept."

- "Collaborate with GPT to develop a series of engaging, interactive activities that introduce students to AI ethics and responsible technology use."

- "Work together with GPT to create a comprehensive resource list for educators interested in integrating AI into their teaching practices."

By applying these strategies and using GPT as a creative partner, Ms. Key was able to develop a captivating TED Talk and an engaging TED-Ed lesson. Over a glass of wine, she shared her experiences with her teacher friends, recounting the moments of vulnerability, humor, and skepticism they had previously discussed. As they listened to her journey, her colleagues began to see the value in embracing AI and GPT, not only as a means of enhancing their teaching practices but also as a way to reignite their passion for education.

Ms. Key's story demonstrates the transformative power of AI-human collaboration. By incorporating these strategies and building a strong partnership with GPT, educators can unlock new levels of creativity, innovation, and passion in their teaching. So, whether you're an educator in a traditional classroom setting, an independent study mentor, or anything in between, don't hesitate to embrace the potential of AI and GPT to enrich your educational journey and the experiences of your students.

Enhancing Communication and Collaboration Among Educators

In today's rapidly evolving world, educators like Ms. Key face a multitude of challenges and opportunities. As they strive to adapt to the diverse needs of their students and navigate the complexities of technology in education, effective communication and collaboration among educators have become more important than ever. In this section, we will explore the various ways that AI technologies, such as GPT, can enhance communication and collaboration among educators like Ms. Key, providing them with real-world examples and tools they can use right away.

One of the significant developments in recent years is the emergence of virtual workshops and webinars, which enabled Ms. Key and educators from around the globe to exchange ideas, best practices, and innovative teaching strategies. With the help of AI, these events can be organized more efficiently and effectively, allowing educators like Ms. Key to learn from one another and grow professionally.

Online discussion forums are another avenue through which educators like Ms. Key can connect and collaborate. AI-powered forums foster more dynamic and engaging conversations among educators, providing them with valuable insights and advice on various aspects of their profession. These forums offer a platform for educators to discuss and address the challenges they face, together.

Collaborative lesson planning is another area where AI technologies like GPT can have a significant impact on educators like Ms. Key. By leveraging AI, educators can create lessons that cater to diverse learning styles and needs, ensuring that no student is left behind. Furthermore, AI can assist in curating and sharing resources more efficiently, allowing educators to access the most up-to-date and high-quality materials.

Peer review and feedback are essential components of professional growth for educators like Ms. Key. With the assistance of AI, such as GPT, educators can refine their work and receive constructive suggestions for improvement. This process helps them elevate their teaching practices and, ultimately, enhance student learning experiences.

As we move along, we will delve deeper into these various applications of AI technologies in enhancing communication and collaboration among educators like Ms. Key. By exploring real-world examples and providing actionable tools and resources, we aim to empower educators to harness the potential of AI, like GPT, to redefine the future of education.

In an increasingly interconnected world, effective communication and collaboration are essential skills for educators like Ms. Key. By leveraging AI technologies like GPT, teachers can foster more productive dialogues, share resources, and enhance their professional networks. In this section, we will explore real-world examples and GPT prompts that can be employed to enrich communication and collaboration among educators like Ms. Key, ultimately leading to more engaging and effective learning experiences for their students.

1. Virtual Workshops and Webinars

Educators like Ms. Key can use GPT-powered platforms to create and participate in virtual workshops and webinars. These online events can facilitate the exchange of best practices, innovative teaching strategies, and valuable resources. For example, Ms. Key could use GPT to generate an engaging presentation on inquiry-based learning, including sample lesson plans and assessment techniques. By sharing her work with colleagues through virtual workshops, she can foster a collaborative atmosphere and inspire other educators.

GPT Prompt: "Create an outline for a presentation on inquiry-based learning, including key concepts, teaching strategies, and assessment techniques."

2. Online Discussion Forums

Ms. Key and many other educators are already using online discussion forums to connect with colleagues from around the world. AI technologies like GPT can enhance these conversations by offering insightful responses to questions, providing feedback on ideas, and even generating new discussion topics. For example, Ms. Key might use GPT to seek advice on incorporating technology in the classroom or addressing a specific challenge she is facing.

GPT Prompt: "Suggest some discussion topics for an online forum on the integration of technology in the classroom."

3. Collaborative Lesson Planning

GPT can be a valuable tool for collaborative lesson planning, helping teachers like Ms. Key create engaging, well-rounded lessons by offering fresh perspectives and new ideas. Ms. Key and her colleagues can input their lesson plan outlines into GPT and receive suggestions for activities, resources, and assessment techniques that cater to diverse learning styles and needs.

GPT Prompt: "Review and suggest improvements for a lesson plan on the American Civil War, focusing on diverse learning styles and engaging activities."

4. Sharing Resources and Best Practices

GPT can help teachers like Ms. Key curate and share resources more efficiently. By inputting keywords or themes related to specific subjects or teaching strategies, she can generate lists of relevant resources, articles, and tools that can be shared within her professional network. This can save time and ensure that teachers have access to the most up-to-date and high-quality materials.

GPT Prompt: "Compile a list of resources related to project-based learning, including articles, tools, and sample lesson plans."

5. Peer Review and Feedback

GPT can assist teachers like Ms. Key in providing constructive feedback on each other's work, such as lesson plans, assessments, or classroom strategies. By analyzing a document and offering suggestions for improvement, GPT can help Ms. Key and her colleagues refine their work and elevate their teaching practices.

GPT Prompt: "Provide feedback on a teacher's lesson plan focusing on environmental sustainability, including suggestions for improvement and additional resources."

By embracing AI technologies like GPT, educators like Ms. Key can foster a more connected and collaborative professional environment. These tools can help teachers expand their networks, share resources, and elevate their teaching practices, ultimately leading to more engaging and effective learning experiences for their students. As Ms.

Key continues her journey, she becomes a pioneer in adopting AI technologies for education, inspiring her colleagues and students alike to explore the transformative power of AI-human collaboration in the classroom.

Maximizing Creativity: Inspiring GPT to Reach New Heights

As Ms. Key continued to experiment with GPT and apply these strategies in her teaching practice, she discovered creative ways to engage her students across various age groups and educational settings. Here are some practical applications for each of the strategies:

1. Details Matter:

In an upper elementary setting, ask GPT to create a detailed lesson plan that incorporates a specific book or topic, catering to the students' interests and learning objectives. For college students, request GPT to generate study guides that focus on key concepts and examples from a particular textbook or lecture series.

2. Open Up Possibilities:

Encourage GPT to generate multiple approaches to teach a complex topic in a middle school setting, such as different perspectives on historical events. For independent study students, have GPT create a variety of project ideas or research questions that explore a specific subject in-depth.

3. Embrace Limits:

In a high school creative writing class, ask GPT to generate story prompts that adhere to a specific genre, theme, or writing style. For college students, request GPT to produce a structured outline for a research paper that focuses on a narrow topic within a broader subject area.

4. Mix and Match:

Have GPT create interdisciplinary lesson plans that combine seemingly unrelated subjects, such as literature and mathematics, for upper elementary or middle school students. For independent study learners, encourage GPT to generate unique research questions that bridge different fields of study.

5. Don't Be Afraid to Tweak:

In a high school setting, iterate and refine GPT-generated lesson plans, incorporating feedback from students and adjusting based on their learning needs. For college students, work with GPT to create multiple drafts of a paper, refining the content and structure with each iteration.

6. Unpredictability is Key:

Introduce surprise elements into GPT-generated activities for upper elementary students, like unexpected twists in a story or unanticipated problem-solving scenarios. For independent study students, provide GPT with random prompts to generate creative research ideas or project concepts.

7. Build Upon GPT's Work:

Use GPT-generated content as a foundation for further exploration and learning in a middle school setting. For example, have students analyze and expand upon GPT-generated historical events or scientific concepts. In a college setting, utilize GPT-generated research outlines as a starting point for more in-depth analysis and exploration.

8. Cross-Pollinate Ideas:

Encourage GPT to draw inspiration from various fields when generating content for high school students, such as integrating artistic principles into a physics lesson. For independent study learners, ask

GPT to develop interdisciplinary projects that combine multiple areas of interest.

9. Question Everything:

In a middle school setting, challenge GPT's assumptions and biases by requesting alternative viewpoints on controversial topics or historical events. For college students, encourage GPT to consider counterarguments and opposing perspectives when generating research papers or essays.

10. Team Up:

Engage GPT in a back-and-forth conversation with students in an upper elementary setting, allowing them to brainstorm ideas and collaborate on a group project. In a college setting, use GPT as a resource for group discussions, encouraging the AI to build upon students' ideas and offer novel perspectives.

By incorporating these strategies into her teaching practice, Ms. Key was able to foster a more dynamic and engaging learning environment. Her students experienced the benefits of AI-human collaboration, which allowed them to explore new creative avenues and expand their understanding of various subjects. As a result, Ms. Key's passion for education was reignited, and her students flourished under her guidance.

In the end, Ms. Key's story serves as a powerful testament to the transformative potential of embracing AI and GPT in education. By applying these strategies and harnessing the full creative potential of GPT, educators can unlock a world of possibilities for their students and themselves. As they share their experiences and insights, they contribute to a growing community of educators who are embracing AI and GPT technologies to revolutionize their teaching practices.

Ms. Key's journey with AI and GPT inspired her to not only write her book but also to take the stage and share her story with a broader audience. As she prepared her TED Talk, "The GPTeacher: Unleashing Creativity in the Classroom," she realized the profound impact these technologies could have on the future of education. In parallel, she began developing a TED-Ed for kids, focusing on the ethical use of AI and its fun applications in learning.

Throughout her journey, Ms. Key has continued to collaborate with her colleagues, exchanging ideas and experiences about implementing AI and GPT in the classroom. Together, they have explored innovative ways to engage students, foster creativity, and break free from the constraints of traditional teaching methods.

By integrating GPT and AI technologies into their teaching practice, these educators are discovering the power of human-AI collaboration, pushing the boundaries of creativity and learning. As more teachers embrace these tools and strategies, they contribute to a collective effort to transform education, empowering students to excel and fostering a more dynamic and engaging learning experience.

The future of education lies in our ability to adapt and innovate, harnessing the potential of AI and GPT technologies while remaining mindful of their limitations and ethical implications. By working together and sharing our knowledge, we can create a future where AI-human collaboration fuels the fire of creativity, inspiring the next generation of learners to reach new heights.

As this chapter of Ms. Key's story comes to an end, it is clear that the journey is just beginning. The integration of AI and GPT technologies in education is an ongoing adventure, filled with opportunities for growth, collaboration, and innovation. As educators, we must continue to explore, experiment, and learn from our experiences, working together to create a brighter future for our students and ourselves. The possibilities are limitless, and the journey has just begun. So, let us embrace AI and GPT as our creative partners, and together, we can change the world.

Ms. Key's Takeaways for Pushing GPT to its Creative Limits

Key Takeaway 1: Experimentation and exploration can help users discover GPT's full creative potential.

GPT Prompts:

a. What are some techniques educators can use to encourage students to explore GPT's capabilities beyond the basics?

b. How can teachers create a learning environment that promotes experimentation and risk-taking with GPT?

c. In what ways can educators support students in pushing GPT's boundaries to unlock new creative possibilities?

d. What are some examples of projects or assignments that challenge students to use GPT in innovative ways?

e. How can teachers help students learn from their failures and iterate on their ideas when working with GPT?

Key Takeaway 2: The quality of GPT's output depends on the clarity and specificity of the input prompts.

GPT Prompts:

a. How can educators teach students to craft effective prompts that yield more creative and relevant results from GPT?

b. What are some strategies for helping students refine their prompts to get better responses from GPT?

c. How can teachers encourage students to experiment with different types of prompts and input formats?

d. In what ways can educators provide feedback on students' prompts to help them improve their GPT interactions?

e. What are some examples of successful prompts that have led to creative and insightful GPT-generated content?

Key Takeaway 3: Iterative conversations with GPT can help users delve deeper into complex topics and generate richer ideas.

GPT Prompts:

a. How can teachers guide students in using iterative conversations with GPT to explore complex subjects and issues?

b. What are some techniques for encouraging students to ask follow-up questions and build on GPT's responses?

c. How can educators help students develop the skills needed to engage in meaningful dialogue with GPT?

d. In what ways can teachers incorporate iterative conversations with GPT into classroom activities and assignments?

e. What are some examples of projects where iterative conversations with GPT have led to deeper understanding or creative breakthroughs?

Key Takeaway 4: Combining GPT's capabilities with other tools and resources can enhance its creative potential.

GPT Prompts:

a. What are some ways educators can encourage students to use GPT in conjunction with other tools and resources?

b. How can teachers help students identify and leverage the strengths of GPT and other tools in their creative projects?

c. What are some examples of successful projects that combine GPT's capabilities with other technologies or resources?

d. How can educators support students in developing the skills needed to integrate GPT and other tools effectively?

e. What are some strategies for fostering a culture of creative collaboration between GPT and other tools in the classroom?

Key Takeaway 5: Reflecting on the creative process with GPT can help users learn from their experiences and grow as creators.

GPT Prompts:

a. How can educators encourage students to reflect on their experiences working with GPT and the creative process?

b. What are some strategies for guiding students in examining the successes and challenges of their GPT interactions?

c. How can teachers help students learn from their GPT experiences and apply those insights to future projects?

d. In what ways can educators incorporate reflection activities into assignments and projects involving GPT?

e. What are some examples of reflection prompts or activities that can help students gain deeper insights into their creative process with GPT?

Chapter 7

Evaluating AI Tools for Education

M s. Key, a firm believer in the potential of AI in education, found herself in the teacher's lounge, sipping coffee with her grade level PLC colleagues. They all taught different subjects, and their opinions about integrating AI into their classrooms varied considerably. Some were skeptics, hesitant to embrace the technology, while others were GPT curious, eager to learn more. Then there were the early adopters, who had already begun incorporating AI tools into their lessons.

As the conversation flowed, Ms. Key noticed that the skeptics expressed concerns about the reliability and security of AI tools. They worried about privacy issues and whether AI could genuinely enhance the learning experience or merely serve as a distraction.

The GPT curious teachers, on the other hand, were intrigued by the possibilities but unsure of where to begin. They had heard about AI's potential in education but needed guidance on how to evaluate AI tools and determine which ones would best suit their teaching styles and subjects.

As always, the early adopters enthusiastically shared their experiences using AI tools in their classrooms. They spoke about the benefits they'd seen firsthand, such as increased student engagement and improved learning outcomes. However, they also acknowledged that choosing the right AI tools and using them effectively required careful consideration and planning.

In addition to the skeptics, GPT curious, and early adopters, there was another category of teacher present in the lounge: the overwhelmed pragmatists. These teachers weren't necessarily opposed to new technology, but they were overworked and overstressed, feeling like they already had too much on their plates. They viewed each new technological development with a mix of exhaustion and resignation, wondering if it was worth investing their limited time and energy into learning about the latest tools, only for them to be replaced by something new down the line.

Overwhelmed pragmatists were typically dedicated educators who wanted to provide the best learning experience for their students, but they often struggled to keep up with the rapid pace of change in the world of educational technology. They longed for stability and consistency and found it challenging to adapt to the constant influx of new tools and teaching methods.

For these teachers, the key to embracing AI in education lay in demonstrating its potential to alleviate some of their workload and streamline their processes, rather than adding another layer of complexity. They needed support and reassurance that investing their time and effort into learning about AI tools would pay off in the long run, ultimately making their jobs more manageable and efficient.

As the discussion unfolded, it became clear that evaluating AI tools for education was a critical aspect of ensuring their successful integration. The conversation that followed delved into various topics, including:

A. Assessing the quality and accuracy of AI-generated content:

How can teachers ensure that the AI tools they use produce reliable and relevant information? What are the best practices for verifying the accuracy of AI-generated content?

B. Privacy and security concerns in AI applications:

What measures should be taken to protect student data when using AI tools? How can educators ensure that the AI tools they use comply with relevant privacy and security regulations?

C. Evaluating the pedagogical value of AI tools:

How can teachers determine if an AI tool aligns with their teaching goals and methodologies? What criteria should be used to assess the tool's effectiveness in enhancing the learning experience?

D. Selecting AI tools that align with educational goals and standards:

How can educators choose AI tools that support their curriculum and adhere to educational standards? What factors should be considered when comparing different AI tools?

E. Integrating AI tools with existing curricula and learning management systems:

How can teachers seamlessly incorporate AI tools into their existing lesson plans and assignments? What strategies can be used to ensure that AI tools complement, rather than disrupt, traditional teaching methods?

As the teachers navigated these topics, they began to realize the importance of evaluating AI tools for education thoroughly. Regardless of their initial stance on AI integration, they all agreed that careful consideration and informed decision-making were crucial to leveraging AI's potential in the classroom. However, the pragmatists were still digging in their heels, not seeing the benefit to their classroom or workload, which was piling up as this meeting dragged on... if only they could come to a consensus on the best AI tools for their independent study school rather than dealing with all the typical traditional school setting literature out there. With a sudden raising of his head, he had an idea. He could stop this discussion and meeting and get back to his actual work if he could show how pointless this all was.

Looking at the instructions still on the board from the earlier professional development session (seriously, how much were they going to cram this down his throat?!), he logged into OpenAI and used ChatGPT-3.5, because there was absolutely no way he was going to drop two Hamiltons on another pointless tech gimmick in GPT-4. Ready to show his colleagues what a useless answer he was sure to get, he typed into the bar, "how do you quickly build consensus around the topic of evaluating ai tools in education?"

Before he could turn his head away, a 7-point plan appeared.

Actual GPT-3.5 response:

Building consensus around the topic of evaluating AI tools in education can be achieved through the following steps:

1. Identify the key stakeholders: Determine who the key stakeholders are in the education system and who would be impacted by the use of AI tools. This includes teachers, students, parents, administrators, and policymakers.

2. Define the evaluation criteria: Define the criteria that will be used to evaluate the AI tools in education. This includes factors such as the accuracy of the AI tool, its effectiveness in achieving learning outcomes, and the ethical considerations related to its use.

3. Communicate the benefits: Communicate the benefits of evaluating AI tools in education to the stakeholders. This includes how it can improve student outcomes, enhance teaching and learning, and make education more efficient.

4. Solicit feedback: Solicit feedback from the stakeholders about their concerns and suggestions related to evaluating AI tools in education.

5. Engage in dialogue: Engage in dialogue with the stakeholders to address their concerns and provide further clarification on the benefits of evaluating AI tools in education.

6. Develop a plan: Develop a plan for evaluating AI tools in education that incorporates the feedback from the stakeholders and aligns with the evaluation criteria.

7. Seek support: Seek support from key influencers in the education system who can help advocate for the evaluation of AI tools in education.

By following these steps, you can quickly build consensus around the topic of evaluating AI tools in education and help ensure that the use of AI tools in education is effective and ethical.

Surprised at how quickly it spat out a reasonable response to his request, the overwhelmed pragmatist held off on raising his objections; still, tl;dr. He was sure that a tougher task would show them that this tool was nothing more than a fancy Google and couldn't handle a real challenge, one that pushed GPT to speak the universal language of teachers: rubrics. He prompted GPT to, "create a rubric to evaluate ai tools for education for an independent study setting" and before he could scoff, boom. There it was:

Actual GPT response:

Sure! Here's a sample rubric to evaluate AI tools for education in an independent study setting:

Criteria 1: Effectiveness (40 points)

- The AI tool must be effective in enhancing learning outcomes and improving student performance.

- The AI tool must provide personalized learning experiences that are tailored to the needs and abilities of individual students.

- The AI tool must be able to identify knowledge gaps and provide targeted feedback and remediation.

Criteria 2: Usability (30 points)

- The AI tool must be easy to use and navigate, and must be accessible to all students regardless of their technical proficiency.

- The AI tool must be compatible with a wide range of devices and platforms, and must work seamlessly with other educational technology tools and resources.

- The AI tool must provide clear instructions and guidance to help students use it effectively.

Criteria 3: Ethics (20 points)

- The AI tool must be developed and implemented with ethical considerations in mind, and must not perpetuate biases or discrimination.

- The AI tool must be transparent in its use of student data, and must protect the privacy and security of that data.

- The AI tool must be subject to ongoing evaluation and improvement to ensure that it continues to meet ethical standards.

Criteria 4: Cost (10 points)

- The AI tool must be cost-effective and provide good value for money.

- The AI tool must be affordable for independent study students and must not create an undue financial burden.

- The AI tool must be sustainable in terms of ongoing maintenance and support costs.

Each criterion is worth a certain number of points, and the rubric can be used to evaluate different AI tools for education in an independent study setting. The total number of points possible is 100.

"Hmph," he muttered to himself with an almost imperceivable head nod, "not bad. But it doesn't *look* like a rubric. I wonder..." he trailed off as he typed, "put this in a table." To his astonishment, with his colleagues still going back and forth about the best course of action, he asked to share his screen. His colleagues, shocked to hear from the person who usually just wants meetings over as quickly as possible, were stunned to see what he pulled up. As they had argued, Mr. Wilson had typed in two prompts to address their entire meeting agenda.

Actual GPT result: *Sure! Here's the rubric in a table format:*

Criteria	Description	Points
Effectiveness	The AI tool must be effective in enhancing learning outcomes and improving student performance. The AI tool must provide personalized learning experiences that are tailored to the needs and abilities of individual students. The AI tool must be able to identify knowledge gaps and provide targeted feedback and remediation.	40
Usability	The AI tool must be easy to use and navigate, and must be accessible to all students regardless of their technical proficiency. The AI tool must be compatible with a wide range of devices and platforms, and must work seamlessly with other educational technology tools and resources. The AI tool must provide clear instructions and guidance to help students use it effectively.	30
Ethics	The AI tool must be developed and implemented with ethical considerations in mind, and must not perpetuate biases or discrimination. The AI tool must be transparent in its use of student data, and must protect the privacy and security of that data. The AI tool must be subject to ongoing evaluation and improvement to ensure that it continues to meet ethical standards.	20
Cost	The AI tool must be cost-effective and provide good value for money. The AI tool must be affordable for independent study students and must not create an undue financial burden. The AI tool must be sustainable in terms of ongoing maintenance and support costs.	10

Seeing the speed and ability to produce exactly what he was looking for with the flick of a wrist was definitely an interesting prospect that moved our once overwhelmed pragmatist into the GPT curious camp, actually ready to give this one a try.

As the group of teachers continued to explore the world of AI in education, they decided to tackle the pressing issue of privacy and security concerns in AI applications. The overwhelmed pragmatist, inspired by the potential benefits of GPT, took the lead in creating a rubric to evaluate AI tools, focusing on the protection of student data.

Safeguarding Student Information

Ms. Key gathered with the skeptics, GPT curious, early adopters, and the overwhelmed pragmatist to discuss how to safeguard student information when using AI tools. Each teacher brought their unique perspective to the conversation, making it a rich and informative discussion.

Ms. Key emphasized the importance of understanding privacy policies and data usage agreements when selecting AI tools for the classroom. The early adopters chimed in, sharing their experiences with different tools and how they had researched the companies behind them to ensure they were compliant with relevant privacy and security regulations.

The GPT curious teachers were eager to learn about encryption and how it could protect student data from unauthorized access. The overwhelmed pragmatist shared a resource on encryption best practices and how to assess the encryption standards used by various AI tools.

The skeptics, always cautious about new technology, raised concerns about potential security breaches and the misuse of student data. They wanted to know how to mitigate these risks and what questions to ask vendors when evaluating AI tools.

In response, the group collaboratively developed a list of essential criteria to consider when assessing the privacy and security aspects of AI tools:

1. Data privacy policies:
Ensure the AI tool provider has a comprehensive privacy policy that outlines how student data is collected, used, and protected.

2. Compliance with regulations:
Verify that the AI tool adheres to relevant privacy and security regulations, such as FERPA, COPPA, and GDPR.

3. Encryption standards:
Check whether the AI tool uses industry-standard encryption methods to protect data both in transit and at rest.

4. Access controls:
Investigate how the AI tool restricts access to student data, and whether it offers role-based access controls for educators and administrators.

5. Data retention and deletion:
Understand the AI tool provider's policies on data retention and deletion, and ensure they align with your school or district's requirements.

6. Third-party sharing:
Determine if the AI tool shares student data with third parties, and if so, under what circumstances and with what protections in place.

7. Security audits and certifications:
Look for evidence of independent security audits or certifications, which can provide added assurance that the AI tool meets industry-standard security practices.

8. Incident response plans:
Ask the AI tool provider about their incident response plan in case of a security breach or data leak, and how they will communicate with affected parties.

By the end of the discussion, the teachers, including the overwhelmed pragmatist, felt more informed and empowered to make responsible decisions when selecting AI tools for their classrooms.

They now had a solid foundation to evaluate AI applications, ensuring that the privacy and security of their students remained a top priority.

Privacy and Security Issues by Grade Band

1. Data privacy policies

Elementary: At this level, it's crucial to find AI tools that have strict policies regarding the collection and use of student data. Younger students may not fully understand the implications of sharing personal information, so it's essential to use tools with age-appropriate privacy settings and clear guidelines.

Middle School: As students grow older, they may begin to use more advanced AI tools. Middle school educators should ensure that these tools have transparent data privacy policies and provide opportunities for students to learn about digital privacy and responsible data sharing.

High School: High school students may use AI tools for more sophisticated tasks like research, collaboration, or test preparation. Educators should prioritize AI tools with robust data privacy policies and promote privacy awareness among their students.

College: At the college level, students may have access to more specialized AI tools for various disciplines. Educators should emphasize the importance of understanding and adhering to the data privacy policies of these tools and encourage students to take responsibility for protecting their personal information.

2. Compliance with regulations

Elementary: It's essential to choose AI tools that comply with child-specific privacy regulations like COPPA in addition to broader regulations like FERPA and GDPR. Educators should be well-versed in these regulations and ensure their chosen tools are compliant.

Middle School: Compliance with privacy regulations remains crucial as students transition from elementary to middle school. Educators should stay up-to-date on any changes to relevant regulations and confirm that their chosen AI tools remain compliant.

High School: High school educators should continue to prioritize compliance with privacy regulations and be prepared to advocate for their students' rights regarding data protection.

College: College educators should ensure that their chosen AI tools comply with any applicable regulations, including those specific to their institution, state, or country. They should also promote awareness among students of their rights and responsibilities related to data privacy.

3. Encryption standards

Elementary: Even for young students, data encryption is vital. Elementary educators should verify that their chosen AI tools use industry-standard encryption methods to protect sensitive information.

Middle School: As students begin to handle more personal and academic data, middle school educators should prioritize AI tools with strong encryption standards.

High School: High school educators should ensure their chosen AI tools maintain high encryption standards and discuss the importance of data encryption with their students.

College: At the college level, students and educators may be handling more sensitive data, making strong encryption standards even more critical. Educators should advocate for the use of AI tools with robust encryption measures and educate students about the importance of data protection.

4. Access controls

Elementary: For younger students, limiting access to their data is essential. Educators should choose AI tools that offer role-based access controls, ensuring that only authorized individuals can access student data.

Middle School: As students grow older and begin to use more advanced AI tools, role-based access controls become increasingly important. Middle school educators should ensure that their chosen tools provide appropriate access controls.

High School: High school educators should prioritize AI tools with granular access controls, allowing them to customize who can access student data and under what circumstances.

College: College educators should seek AI tools that offer advanced access controls, enabling them to manage access to sensitive information according to the specific needs of their courses and institutions.

5. Data retention and deletion

Elementary: It's crucial to understand AI tool providers' policies on data retention and deletion at the elementary level. Educators should select tools that align with their school or district's requirements and teach students about the importance of managing their digital footprints.

Middle School: Middle school educators should continue to prioritize data retention and deletion policies, ensuring that their chosen AI tools align with their institution's guidelines.

High School: High school educators should educate students about the long-term implications of data retention and deletion policies and ensure that their chosen AI tools adhere to best practices for managing student data.

College: College educators should carefully review AI tool providers' data retention and deletion policies to ensure they comply with institutional, state, and federal guidelines. They should also promote awareness among students of the importance of understanding and managing their digital footprints.

6. Third-party sharing policies

Elementary: Educators should select AI tools that have strict policies against sharing student data with third parties without proper consent. They should also teach young students about the risks associated with data sharing.

Middle School: Middle school educators should prioritize AI tools with clear third-party sharing policies, and continue to educate students about responsible data sharing practices.

High School: High school educators should ensure that their chosen AI tools have robust third-party sharing policies and discuss the implications of data sharing with their students.

College: College educators should choose AI tools with transparent third-party sharing policies and encourage students to be proactive in understanding how their data may be shared or used.

7. Anonymization of data

Elementary: It's essential to choose AI tools that anonymize student data whenever possible. Educators should explain the concept of data anonymization to young students and discuss its importance in protecting their privacy.

Middle School: As students begin to use more advanced AI tools, anonymization becomes increasingly important. Middle school educators should prioritize tools that anonymize student data and teach students about the benefits of data anonymization.

High School: High school educators should continue to emphasize the importance of data anonymization and ensure that their chosen AI tools follow best practices for anonymizing student data.

College: At the college level, educators should advocate for the use of AI tools that prioritize data anonymization and promote awareness among students of the importance of protecting their personal information.

8. Regular security audits and updates

Elementary: Educators should select AI tools that undergo regular security audits and updates to ensure the protection of student data. They should also teach young students about the importance of keeping their devices and software up-to-date.

Middle School: Middle school educators should continue to prioritize AI tools with regular security audits and updates and educate students on the importance of maintaining their digital security.

High School: High school educators should ensure that their chosen AI tools maintain high security standards through regular audits and updates and discuss the significance of digital security with their students.

College: College educators should seek AI tools that undergo rigorous security audits and updates and encourage students to take responsibility for their digital security by keeping their devices and software up-to-date.

Clearly, protecting student privacy and ensuring security when using AI tools in education is crucial at all levels, from elementary school to college. By considering factors such as data collection, storage, and deletion practices, third-party sharing policies, anonymization of data, and regular security audits and updates, educators can make informed decisions when selecting AI tools for their classrooms.

As the cast of teachers, including the overwhelmed pragmatist, become more aware of privacy and security concerns, they also recognize the importance of evaluating the pedagogical value of AI tools. Choosing AI tools that support learning objectives and foster student engagement is a crucial aspect of successfully integrating AI into the classroom.

In the next section, we will delve deeper into the criteria educators should consider when evaluating the pedagogical value of AI tools. We will explore factors such as alignment with learning objectives, adaptability, student engagement, accessibility, and user feedback, providing guidance for each teacher type in our cast as they navigate the world of AI in education. This will enable them to make informed decisions and ultimately enhance the learning experiences of their students through the effective use of AI technology.

Evaluating the Pedagogical Value of AI Tools

Ms. Key sat at her desk, reviewing her lesson plans and pondering how AI tools could enhance her students' learning experiences. She had learned so much about AI's potential and how it could be harnessed for educational purposes, but she also knew that not all AI tools were created equal. It was crucial to evaluate the pedagogical value of these tools to ensure they genuinely supported her learning objectives and fostered student engagement.

Later that week, Ms. Key gathered with her fellow teachers, including the skeptic, the GPT-curious, the early adopter, and the overwhelmed pragmatist, for their regular meeting. She brought up the topic of evaluating the pedagogical value of AI tools, knowing that each of her colleagues had different perspectives and experiences. Their lively conversation touched on several essential points that educators should consider when selecting AI tools for their classrooms:

1. Alignment with learning objectives:

The AI tool should support and enhance the learning objectives set for the students, rather than distract or detract from them.

2. Adaptability:

The tool should be able to adapt to individual students' needs and learning styles, providing personalized support and feedback.

3. Student engagement:

The AI tool should foster student engagement, curiosity, and motivation, promoting active learning and collaboration.

4. Accessibility:

The tool should be accessible to all students, regardless of their socioeconomic status, language, or disability, ensuring that no one is left behind.

5. User feedback:

Educators should consider feedback from other teachers and students who have used the AI tool to gain insight into its effectiveness and potential drawbacks.

As the meeting concluded, Ms. Key and her colleagues felt more empowered to make informed decisions about incorporating AI tools into their classrooms. They understood the importance of evaluating the pedagogical value of these tools to ensure they supported their teaching goals and provided meaningful learning experiences for their students. Each teacher, regardless of their initial stance on AI in education, left the meeting eager to explore the potential of AI tools in their classrooms and committed to choosing those that best aligned with their students' needs and learning objectives.

Each teacher took on a different aspect of evaluating the pedagogical value of AI tools, and they reconvened to share their findings. They each came up with three GPT prompt suggestions to help them tackle their respective issues:

Skeptic (Alignment with learning objectives):

The skeptic teacher focused on finding examples of user feedback that highlighted how well AI tools aligned with learning objectives. They discovered that some AI tools were praised for providing targeted support for specific skills and concepts, while others received criticism for being too generic or disconnected from curriculum standards. This teacher learned that examining user feedback can help educators identify AI tools that are most effective in reinforcing learning objectives.

1. How can AI tools be used to reinforce learning objectives in a middle school math class, while also maintaining student engagement?

2. What are some ways AI tools can help students achieve specific learning objectives in a language arts class?

3. How can I ensure that AI tools used in my science class align with the curriculum standards and learning goals?

GPT-curious (Adaptability):

The GPT-curious teacher looked for user feedback that showcased the adaptability of AI tools in meeting diverse student needs. They found testimonials from educators who appreciated AI tools that offered personalized learning paths, accommodated different learning styles, and adjusted to the learner's pace. This teacher realized that user feedback could provide insights into the flexibility of AI tools and their potential to cater to different learning needs.

1. How can AI tools be customized to accommodate the individual learning needs and preferences of students in a diverse classroom?

2. What are some AI-driven adaptive learning platforms that offer personalized feedback and support for students?

3. How can I use AI tools to differentiate instruction and assessment in my history class?

Early Adopter (Student engagement):

The early adopter teacher sought user feedback that highlighted the impact of AI tools on student engagement. They discovered that some AI tools received high praise for their ability to make learning fun, interactive, and relevant, while others were critiqued for being uninteresting or difficult to navigate. This teacher learned that user feedback could help identify AI tools that effectively boost student engagement and motivation.

1. How can AI tools be incorporated into project-based learning activities to promote student engagement and collaboration?

2. What are some examples of AI-driven educational games that encourage active learning in various subject areas?

3. How can AI-powered chatbots be used to facilitate peer-to-peer learning and student-driven discussions in an online learning environment?

Overwhelmed Pragmatist (Accessibility):

The overwhelmed pragmatist teacher focused on user feedback regarding the accessibility of AI tools. They found comments from educators who appreciated AI tools that were easy to use, provided clear instructions, and offered support for students with disabilities. This teacher realized that user feedback could help them identify AI tools that were accessible and user-friendly for all students, regardless of their abilities or background.

1. What measures can be taken to ensure AI tools are accessible to students with disabilities, including those with visual or hearing impairments?

2. How can I find AI tools that offer multilingual support for students who are English language learners?

3. What are some strategies for acquiring and implementing AI tools in schools with limited resources or budgets?

By working together on the user feedback category, the teachers were able to connect their own perspectives with the research findings. This collaborative approach allowed them to gain a deeper understanding of the significance of user feedback when evaluating the pedagogical value of AI tools. Armed with this knowledge, they felt more prepared to make informed decisions when selecting AI tools for their classrooms.

Each teacher took note of the prompt suggestions provided by their peers, eager to explore the potential of AI tools in their respective areas. By sharing their expertise and insights, they all gained a deeper understanding of how to evaluate the pedagogical value of AI tools and how these tools could benefit their students.

As the teachers continued their exploration of AI tools, they started to focus on selecting AI tools that aligned with educational goals and standards, as well as integrating these tools with existing curricula and learning management systems. Through their collaborative research and the helpful insights provided by GPT, they began to see the potential benefits that AI tools could bring to their classrooms.

Selecting AI Tools that Align with Educational Goals and Standards

One afternoon, Ms. Key gathered her colleagues in the school library to discuss their experiences and insights on selecting AI tools that aligned with their educational goals and standards. As each teacher shared their thoughts, they found that AI tools could indeed support various learning objectives and help students develop essential skills.

The skeptic teacher, who initially doubted the effectiveness of AI tools, was pleasantly surprised to discover that certain AI tools were specifically designed to target particular learning objectives and curriculum standards. They learned that by carefully selecting AI tools that aligned with their educational goals, they could enhance their students' learning experiences.

The overwhelmed pragmatist teacher, who was initially hesitant about adopting new technologies, found that some AI tools made it easy for them to track students' progress and adjust their teaching strategies accordingly. They realized that AI tools could help them better support their students in reaching educational goals and meeting standards.

Integrating AI Tools with Existing Curricula and Learning Management Systems

The discussion then shifted to the topic of integrating AI tools with existing curricula and learning management systems. The GPT-curious teacher shared their experience of using AI tools that seamlessly integrated with their current teaching resources and systems. They found that some AI tools could complement their lesson plans and provide additional support for students, without requiring significant changes to their existing curriculum.

The early adopter teacher, who had more experience with AI tools, shared examples of tools that could easily be integrated with popular learning management systems, such as Google Classroom or Canvas. They emphasized the importance of choosing AI tools that were compatible with their school's infrastructure, making it easier for both teachers and students to adopt and use these tools effectively.

As the teachers continued their collaborative exploration, they became increasingly convinced of the potential benefits of AI tools in education. Even the most skeptical and overwhelmed among them started to recognize the value of these tools in supporting their teaching and enhancing their students' learning experiences. By focusing on selecting AI tools that aligned with educational goals and standards, and integrating them with existing curricula and learning management systems, the teachers felt more confident and better equipped to embrace the exciting possibilities offered by AI in education.

As the chapter drew to a close, the teachers found themselves gathered once more in the school library, reflecting on their journey of evaluating AI tools for education. Ms. Key, who had been an avid proponent of AI from the beginning, couldn't help but feel proud of the progress they had made together.

Their collaborative research and shared experiences had led them to gain valuable insights into privacy and security concerns, evaluating the pedagogical value of AI tools, and selecting AI tools that align with educational goals and standards, as well as integrating them with existing curricula and learning management systems.

The skeptic teacher, who had initially been wary of AI, was now more open to experimenting with AI tools in the classroom. The overwhelmed pragmatist, once resistant to change, had discovered that some AI tools could actually save them time and effort, while providing valuable support for their students. The GPT-curious teacher had become even more eager to explore the potential of AI, and the early adopter teacher was keen on sharing their knowledge and experiences with their colleagues.

As the teachers left the library, they knew that their journey of embracing AI in education was far from over. They understood that it would require ongoing effort, continued learning, and adaptation as technology evolved. However, they were now better prepared to face the challenges ahead and make informed decisions about implementing AI tools in their classrooms.

With a renewed sense of enthusiasm and optimism, Ms. Key and her colleagues embarked on the next chapter of their AI-driven educational adventure, knowing that they had the support and camaraderie of their fellow teachers. Together, they were determined to harness the power of AI to create a better, more engaging, and fulfilling learning experience for their students.

Ms. Key's Takeaways for Evaluating AI Tools for Education

Key Takeaway 1: Understanding the importance of evaluating AI tools for effectiveness and ethical considerations.

GPT Prompts:

a. What are the essential factors teachers should consider when selecting AI tools for their classrooms?

b. How can educators ensure that the AI tools they use meet ethical standards and protect student data?

c. What are some methods educators can use to compare and contrast different AI tools based on their pedagogical value?

d. How can schools and districts create guidelines to help teachers evaluate AI tools for education?

e. What are the potential risks and consequences of not thoroughly evaluating AI tools before implementing them in the classroom?

Key Takeaway 2: Evaluating AI tools based on privacy and security concerns.

GPT Prompts:

a. What steps can educators take to ensure that AI tools protect student privacy and adhere to relevant regulations?

b. How can teachers work with IT departments and administrators to address privacy and security concerns related to AI tools?

c. What questions should educators ask AI tool vendors to assess their commitment to privacy and security?

d. How can schools and districts develop policies to guide the use of AI tools while maintaining student privacy?

e. What are some ways educators can educate students about the importance of privacy and security in the context of AI?

Key Takeaway 3: Assessing the pedagogical value of AI tools.

GPT Prompts:

a. What criteria should teachers use to evaluate the instructional effectiveness of AI tools?

b. How can educators determine whether an AI tool aligns with their educational goals and curriculum standards?

c. What are some strategies for integrating AI tools into existing lesson plans and activities?

d. How can teachers assess the impact of AI tools on student learning outcomes and engagement?

e. What are some methods for gathering feedback from students and colleagues to inform the selection and use of AI tools?

Key Takeaway 4: Selecting AI tools that align with educational goals and standards.

GPT Prompts:

a. How can teachers ensure that AI tools support and enhance their instructional objectives and strategies?

b. What are some ways educators can align AI tools with curriculum standards and learning goals?

c. How can teachers collaborate with colleagues and experts to identify AI tools that support best practices in teaching and learning?

d. In what ways can educators use AI tools to differentiate instruction and meet the diverse needs of their students?

e. How can teachers track the effectiveness of AI tools in supporting student learning and make data-informed decisions about their use?

Key Takeaway 5: Integrating AI tools with existing curricula and learning management systems.

GPT Prompts:

a. What are some strategies for seamlessly incorporating AI tools into existing classroom routines and learning environments?

b. How can educators leverage AI tools to support blended learning and technology-enhanced instruction?

c. In what ways can teachers use AI tools to streamline classroom management and administrative tasks?

d. How can educators collaborate with IT departments to ensure the successful integration of AI tools with learning management systems?

e. What are some professional development opportunities available for educators to learn about integrating AI tools into their classrooms?

Chapter 8

Integrating AI into the Classroom and Beyond

As the summer sun shone brightly outside, Ms. Key found herself immersed in planning for the upcoming school year. She was determined to create an AI-enhanced learning environment that would inspire her students and encourage collaboration. In the past, her classroom had been a place where students worked together, problem-solved, and learned through traditional methods. But she was excited about the possibilities that AI technology could bring to her teaching practice, particularly in terms of fostering an even more collaborative and engaging atmosphere.

Ms. Key knew that integrating AI tools into her classroom would be a significant shift for her and her students, but she was motivated by the potential benefits it could offer. As she prepared for this transition, she sought to create a classroom that would not only integrate AI effectively but also provide a rich, collaborative learning experience for her students

In the quiet of her home office, surrounded by colorful posters and various educational resources, she considered the key components of a collaborative AI-enhanced classroom. She thought about the conversations she had had with her colleagues, reflecting on the mix of enthusiasm, curiosity, skepticism, and pragmatism they had exhibited when discussing AI in education. Ms. Key knew that she would need to address a wide range of perspectives and concerns as she planned her classroom, ensuring that her students, their parents, and her fellow educators would feel comfortable and supported in this new learning environment.

She began by identifying the core principles that she wanted her AI-enhanced classroom to embody: collaboration, problem-solving, creativity, and a growth mindset. These principles would guide her decision-making as she explored various AI tools and designed her curriculum for the school year.

Next, Ms. Key turned her attention to the practical aspects of her AI-enhanced classroom. She considered how to provide equitable access to AI tools and resources for all her students, regardless of their socioeconomic background or digital literacy. She brainstormed ways to involve her fellow educators in her AI-driven classroom, providing professional development opportunities and encouraging collaboration across disciplines.

She also thought about the balance she would need to strike between the roles of teachers, students, and AI tools in her classroom. She knew that she would need to adapt her teaching methods and expectations, allowing AI to augment her students' learning experiences while still providing the guidance, support, and human connection that they needed to succeed.

As she delved deeper into her planning, Ms. Key began to envision her AI-enhanced classroom as a vibrant, dynamic space where students would work together on projects, using AI tools to generate ideas, create visual representations, and refine their work collaboratively. She imagined her students developing teamwork and problem-solving skills through AI-driven projects, learning how to leverage AI tools in the context of real-world challenges, and cultivating a growth mindset that would serve them well in an increasingly technology-driven world.

As the summer days continued to pass, Ms. Key's excitement for the new school year grew. She was confident that her carefully planned AI-enhanced learning environment would engage and inspire her students, fostering collaboration, creativity, and a love of learning that would prepare them for a future shaped by AI. With a sense of anticipation and optimism, she eagerly awaited the first day of school, ready to embark on a new journey with her students in their AI-enhanced classroom.

As Ms. Key delved deeper into her research, she discovered a wealth of AI tools designed to encourage collaboration among students. These tools had the potential to transform her classroom into a dynamic, engaging, and inclusive learning environment where every student had a chance to contribute and develop their skills.

She began to explore AI tools that supported real-time collaboration, enabling students to work together on documents, presentations, and other projects, no matter where they were. Tools like Google Workspace, Microsoft Teams, and other cloud-based platforms offered a range of collaborative features, including file sharing, synchronous editing, and integrated communication channels. By using these tools, Ms. Key's students could collaborate on assignments, share resources, and communicate with one another seamlessly.

Another area that caught Ms. Key's attention was AI-driven brainstorming and ideation tools. She discovered platforms like Miro, which provided students with an interactive, virtual whiteboard where they could visualize their thoughts, generate ideas, and collaborate on project planning. She also found tools like ChatGPT, which could be used to inspire students by generating prompts, questions, and ideas that they could then discuss and build upon together.

Ms. Key also explored the potential of AI tools in facilitating peer feedback and assessment. She came across platforms like Peergrade, which allowed students to submit their work and receive feedback from their classmates based on specific criteria. This not only encouraged collaboration but also helped students develop critical thinking and evaluation skills.

As she considered the various AI tools available, Ms. Key started to envision how these tools could be integrated into her classroom to promote collaboration and engagement. For instance, she could assign group projects where students would use AI-driven ideation tools to brainstorm ideas and develop a project plan. They could then work together using cloud-based collaboration platforms to create and refine their work, communicating through integrated chat and video conferencing tools. Finally, students could use peer assessment tools to provide feedback on each other's work, fostering a supportive and collaborative learning environment.

To ensure that the AI tools she chose were accessible and inclusive, Ms. Key focused on finding platforms that offered customizable features, such as adjustable font sizes, text-to-speech capabilities, and translation options. This would allow her to cater to the diverse needs of her students, ensuring that everyone could participate and collaborate effectively.

As her plans for an AI-enhanced collaborative classroom began to take shape, Ms. Key realized the importance of teaching her students the necessary digital literacy skills to use these tools effectively. She decided to dedicate time at the beginning of the school year to teaching her students how to navigate and use the various AI tools they would be utilizing in class. This would not only empower her students to collaborate effectively but also help them develop valuable digital skills that they could carry with them into their future education and careers.

Ms. Key recognized the need to create a supportive and trusting classroom culture in which her students felt comfortable sharing their ideas and collaborating with their peers. She planned to incorporate team-building activities and icebreakers at the beginning of the school year to help her students get to know one another and establish a sense of community. She would also emphasize the importance of respecting diverse perspectives, valuing everyone's contributions, and practicing active listening and empathy.

By the end of the summer, Ms. Key had crafted an AI-enhanced collaborative classroom that she was excited to implement in the coming school year. She felt confident that her students would benefit from the opportunities provided by these AI tools, developing essential teamwork, problem-solving, and communication skills in a supportive and engaging learning environment.

With her plans in place and her AI tools selected, Ms. Key eagerly awaited the first day of school, ready to embark on a new journey with her students as they explored the potential of AI-driven collaboration and creativity.

Integrating GPT into Grade-Level Bands

Let's take a look at some grade-level specific ideas for integrating GPT and AI into your classroom:

Elementary School:

1. Use GPT to generate engaging story prompts for creative writing assignments.

a. "Generate 5 story prompts involving magical creatures and their adventures."

b. "Create 3 story prompts where a young protagonist uses their creativity to solve a problem."

c. "Provide 4 story prompts that teach a valuable lesson about friendship and teamwork."

2. Create AI-generated math puzzles and problem-solving activities tailored to the class's skill level.

a. "Design 5 math puzzles for 3rd graders that involve addition and subtraction within 100."

b. "Generate 3 engaging word problems that require students to use multiplication and division."

c. "Create 4 geometry-based activities to help students understand basic shapes and their properties."

3. Use GPT to generate historical or cultural facts for students to research and present to the class.

a. "Provide 5 interesting facts about ancient civilizations for students to explore further."

b. "List 4 significant events in American history for students to research and present."

c. "Suggest 3 fascinating cultural practices from around the world for students to investigate."

4. Incorporate AI-generated art project ideas or craft suggestions for hands-on learning experiences.

a. "Generate 3 art projects that incorporate recycled materials and promote environmental awareness."

b. "Create 4 craft ideas that celebrate cultural diversity and encourage students to explore different traditions."

c. "Provide 5 hands-on activities to teach students about famous artists and their techniques."

Middle School:

1. Use GPT to suggest debate topics or discussion questions related to current events or course material.

a. "List 4 debate topics related to the impact of technology on society."

b. "Generate 3 discussion questions about the role of social media in shaping public opinion."

c. "Suggest 5 thought-provoking questions about the influence of advertising on consumer behavior."

2. Collaborate with AI to create interactive quizzes or games for students to review course content.

a. "Design an interactive quiz on the major themes and characters of a novel studied in class."

b. "Create a game that reinforces understanding of key scientific concepts, such as photosynthesis or the water cycle."

c. "Generate a trivia challenge that covers important historical events and figures from a specific time period."

3. Use GPT-generated prompts to facilitate group discussions on social-emotional learning topics.

a. "Provide 3 prompts to encourage conversations about empathy and understanding different perspectives."

b. "Create 4 discussion starters on the importance of resilience and overcoming obstacles."

c. "Generate 5 conversation prompts about the role of teamwork and collaboration in problem-solving."

4. Assign AI-generated research questions for students to explore and present their findings.

a. "Suggest 3 research questions about the impact of climate change on ecosystems."

b. "Generate 4 inquiry questions related to the development of renewable energy sources."

c. "Provide 5 research topics exploring the relationship between mental health and social media use."

High School:

1. Incorporate GPT-generated prompts for essay topics or research projects, allowing students to choose the one that interests them the most.

a. "List 4 essay topics that analyze the role of technology in modern society."

b. "Generate 3 research project ideas related to the impact of globalization on culture and the economy."

c. "Suggest 5 essay prompts that explore the ethical implications of advancements in artificial intelligence."

2. Use GPT to provide personalized writing feedback and suggestions for improvement.

a. "Review this student essay and provide specific feedback on how to improve clarity and organization."

b. "Analyze this narrative piece and offer suggestions to include more descriptive language."

c. "Examine this persuasive essay and recommend ways to strengthen the argument and evidence."

3. Have students collaborate with AI to create multimedia presentations or video projects.

a. "Generate a storyboard for a short video explaining the causes and effects of climate change."

b. "Create a script for a podcast episode discussing the pros and cons of social media."

c. "Provide an outline for a presentation on the history and impact of a significant technological invention."

4. Assign GPT-generated STEM challenges, allowing students to develop their problem-solving skills.

a. "Design a physics-based challenge that requires students to apply their knowledge of force and motion."

b. "Create a chemistry experiment to explore the properties of different substances and their reactions."

c. "Generate a coding challenge that encourages students to develop their programming skills and create a simple game."

Independent Study:

1. Use GPT to generate self-paced learning resources, such as reading materials, videos, or interactive activities.

a. "Compile a list of 5 articles, videos, or podcasts related to the impact of technology on mental health."

b. "Create a set of interactive activities to help students practice their foreign language skills."

c. "Provide a curated list of documentaries and films related to a specific historical period or event."

2. Collaborate with AI to create personalized study plans or learning objectives.

a. "Develop a study plan for a student aiming to improve their math skills in preparation for an upcoming exam."

b. "Create a set of personalized learning objectives for a student interested in exploring a specific scientific field."

c. "Design a reading list and schedule for a student seeking to expand their knowledge of world literature."

3. Use GPT to suggest real-world projects or challenges for students to tackle independently.

a. "Generate a list of 3 hands-on engineering projects for students to build and test their own inventions."

b. "Suggest 4 ideas for community service projects that students can lead to address local issues."

c. "Provide 5 creative prompts for students to develop their own artistic portfolio or body of work."

4. Implement AI-generated self-assessment tools to monitor progress and adjust learning goals accordingly.

a. "Design a self-assessment questionnaire for students to reflect on their progress in mastering a specific skill."

b. "Create a set of reflection prompts to help students evaluate their growth and development in a specific subject area."

c. "Generate a progress tracker for students to monitor their achievements and adjust their learning goals as needed."

College:

1. Use GPT to facilitate peer review or collaborative writing projects among students.

a. "Generate a set of guidelines for peer review, focusing on providing constructive feedback and supporting each other's growth as writers."

b. "Create a collaborative writing prompt that encourages students to work together to develop a cohesive narrative or argument."

c. "Provide a set of discussion questions for students to explore as they work together on a group research project."

2. Incorporate AI-generated case studies or simulations to enhance learning in specific subject areas.

a. "Design a business case study that challenges students to analyze and solve a real-world problem."

b. "Create a simulation activity for students to explore the effects of policy decisions on a nation's economy."

c. "Generate a hypothetical scenario for students to apply their knowledge of psychology in a clinical setting."

   3. Use GPT to suggest innovative research questions or project ideas for students to pursue.

a. "Provide a list of 5 cutting-edge research questions in the field of artificial intelligence and machine learning."

b. "Suggest 3 interdisciplinary project ideas that combine elements of science, technology, and the humanities."

c. "Generate 4 innovative research topics related to the intersection of environmental sustainability and urban planning."

   4. Assign GPT-generated prompts for reflective writing or journaling to promote self-awareness and personal growth.

a. "Create a set of journal prompts to help students reflect on their values, strengths, and areas for growth."

b. "Design a series of reflective writing exercises to encourage students to explore their personal and professional goals."

c. "Provide a list of thought-provoking questions for students to contemplate as they navigate the challenges and opportunities of college life."

Using GPT to Organize and De-stress

Finally, let's examine some of the ways the GPT can make your busy life less stressful, allowing you more time to do the things you love, be it gardening, binging a show, catching up with friends, spending time with family, or even writing a book!

1. Use GPT to generate a list of organizational tools and strategies tailored to your teaching style and classroom needs.

- "Suggest a list of top 10 organizational tools and strategies that can help me streamline my classroom management and workflow."

- "Provide a set of teaching tools and strategies that can enhance productivity and organization in a project-based learning environment."

- "Recommend effective classroom organization techniques for managing a diverse group of students with various learning needs."

2. Collaborate with AI to create a personalized professional development plan, including goals, learning resources, and a timeline.

- "Help me create a professional development plan focused on integrating technology and AI in the classroom, including goals, resources, and a timeline."

- "Assist me in developing a personalized plan for improving my classroom management skills, including objectives, learning materials, and milestones."

- "Guide me in designing a professional growth plan centered on fostering student engagement and motivation, with clear goals, resources, and a schedule."

3. Use GPT to design engaging and innovative lesson plans or curriculum materials for the upcoming school year.

- "Generate a series of lesson plans incorporating AI technology to enhance student learning and engagement in a middle school science class."

- "Create a unit plan focused on exploring multicultural literature in a high school English class, incorporating interactive and innovative learning activities."

- "Design a set of hands-on, inquiry-based lessons for an elementary school math class, emphasizing real-world problem-solving and collaboration."

4. Generate AI-assisted templates for parent-teacher communication, such as newsletters, progress reports, and email updates.

- "Create a template for a visually appealing and informative monthly classroom newsletter to share with parents."

- "Design a progress report template that effectively communicates student strengths, areas for improvement, and strategies for growth."

- "Provide an email template for efficiently updating parents on upcoming events, assignments, and classroom news."

5. Collaborate with GPT to create an organized digital filing system for lesson plans, student work, and other essential teaching materials.

- "Help me develop a digital filing system for organizing and managing my lesson plans, student work, and resources using cloud storage."

- "Assist me in creating an efficient system for categorizing and archiving instructional materials and assessments using an online platform."

- "Guide me in setting up a user-friendly digital organization system for tracking student progress and maintaining a record of parent communication."

6. Use GPT to generate ideas for classroom decorations or themes that inspire creativity and a love for learning.

- "Suggest a list of creative and inspiring classroom themes that foster a positive learning environment for elementary school students."

- "Generate ideas for engaging and interactive classroom decorations that promote collaboration and critical thinking in a middle school setting."

- "Provide suggestions for innovative and visually appealing classroom design elements that support a growth mindset and a love for learning in high school students."

7. Explore GPT-generated suggestions for self-care and wellness practices, ensuring you return to the classroom refreshed and ready to inspire your students.

- "Provide a list of self-care practices and wellness activities specifically tailored to the needs and challenges of educators."

- "Suggest a variety of mindfulness and stress reduction techniques that can help teachers maintain a healthy work-life balance."

- "Offer recommendations for rejuvenating summer activities and hobbies that can help teachers recharge and refocus for the upcoming school year."

Ms. Key's Takeaways for Integrating AI into the Classroom

Ms. Key reflected on her journey of integrating AI tools into her classroom and the key takeaways she had gleaned from the experience. She felt that these important lessons could help other educators who were considering using AI tools in their own classrooms:

Key Takeaway 1: AI tools can foster collaboration and engagement among students.

GPT Prompts:

a. How can AI tools improve collaboration in group projects?

b. In what ways do AI tools promote student engagement?

c. How can AI-driven ideation tools spark creativity in collaborative tasks?

d. What are some examples of AI tools that encourage real-time collaboration?

e. How can AI tools help students develop better communication skills?

Key Takeaway 2: Selecting accessible and inclusive AI tools is crucial for meeting diverse student needs.

GPT Prompts:

a. What features should educators look for in accessible AI tools?

b. How can inclusive AI tools help support students with different learning needs?

c. Why is it important to choose AI tools that offer customization options?

d. How can translation features in AI tools promote inclusivity in the classroom?

e. How do adjustable font sizes and text-to-speech capabilities make AI tools more accessible?

Key Takeaway 3: Teaching digital literacy skills is essential for effective AI-enhanced collaboration.

GPT Prompts:

a. Why is it important to teach students digital literacy skills when using AI tools?

b. What are some effective ways to teach students how to navigate and use AI tools?

c. How can digital literacy skills benefit students in their future education and careers?

d. How can educators help students develop responsible and ethical AI usage habits?

e. What challenges might students face when learning to use AI tools, and how can educators address them?

Key Takeaway 4: Building a supportive and trusting classroom culture is key to successful AI-enhanced collaboration.

GPT Prompts:

a. How can educators create a positive and inclusive classroom environment for AI-enhanced collaboration?

b. What are some team-building activities that can help foster a sense of community among students?

c. How can educators encourage active listening and empathy in an AI-enhanced classroom?

d. Why is it important to value diverse perspectives when using AI tools for collaboration?

e. How can educators model respectful behavior when using AI tools in the classroom?

Key Takeaway 5: Balancing the roles of teachers, students, and AI tools is crucial for an effective AI-enhanced learning environment.

GPT Prompts:

a. How can teachers maintain their role as facilitators and guides in an AI-enhanced classroom?

b. In what ways can students take responsibility for their learning in an AI-driven environment?

c. How can educators ensure that AI tools complement, rather than replace, traditional teaching methods?

d. What are the potential challenges of balancing the roles of teachers, students, and AI tools?

e. How can educators evaluate the effectiveness of AI tools in supporting their teaching goals and strategies?

With these key takeaways in mind, Ms. Key felt prepared to tackle the challenges and opportunities presented by an AI-enhanced collaborative classroom, confident that her students would benefit from the engaging and supportive learning environment she had created.

Chapter 9

Looking Forward

The Future of AI in Education

With a steaming cup of liquid happiness in hand, Ms. Key settled into her favorite armchair, a stack of books and articles on AI in education piled high beside her. As she glanced through the titles, she couldn't help but feel a sense of excitement and anticipation for the future of AI in education. It was clear that the landscape of teaching and learning was evolving at a rapid pace, and she knew that it was her responsibility to ensure that she and her students were well-prepared to navigate this brave new world.

AI literacy for educators and students

Ms. Key understood that the foundation of this preparation lay in developing AI literacy for both educators and students. She envisioned a future where AI tools were seamlessly integrated into the curriculum, providing a wealth of opportunities for learning and collaboration. By fostering an understanding of AI's capabilities, limitations, and potential applications, she knew that her students would be better equipped to harness the power of this technology in their academic and professional lives.

Bridging the digital divide: Ensuring equal access to AI tools

As she sipped her tea, Ms. Key thought about the importance of bridging the digital divide and ensuring equal access to AI tools for all students. She recognized that students from different backgrounds and socio-economic statuses might not have the same opportunities to engage with AI, which could lead to an even greater disparity in educational outcomes. Determined to address this issue, she began to brainstorm ways to promote digital equity and make AI tools accessible to every student in her classroom.

Teacher professional development in AI

Ms. Key knew that she wasn't alone in her quest to embrace AI in education. Across the globe, teachers were seeking to develop their understanding of this groundbreaking technology, eager to stay informed and adapt their teaching methods accordingly. She considered the importance of ongoing professional development in AI, recognizing that a community of like-minded educators could offer invaluable support, resources, and inspiration as they navigated this ever-changing landscape together.

Preparing students for careers in AI and related fields

As her gaze drifted toward the window, Ms. Key pondered the future careers of her students. She knew that many of them would one day work in AI and related fields, shaping the trajectory of this technology and driving innovation across industries. By providing them with a strong foundation in AI literacy, fostering their creativity and problem-solving skills, and encouraging them to explore careers in AI, she was confident that she could help her students become the leaders and trailblazers of tomorrow.

The future of AI in education: Opportunities and challenges

Ms. Key was under no illusion that the journey ahead would be without its challenges. She acknowledged that the rapid advancement of AI technology could bring with it unforeseen consequences, ethical dilemmas, and changes to the role of the educator. However, she also saw a wealth of opportunities and potential for growth, as AI continued to revolutionize the way we teach and learn.

With a renewed sense of purpose, Ms. Key set her empty teacup aside and picked up the first book from her stack, ready to dive deeper into the world of AI in education. As she turned the pages, she was filled with excitement and determination, eager to share her new-found knowledge with her students and empower them to embrace an AI-driven future with confidence and curiosity.

AI Literacy in the Current Landscape

It's lovely that Ms. Key is getting this all figured out, but what does AI literacy look like for you and your students? Let's take a look, starting with elementary and building on the skills from there as students progress through K-12 and beyond, as well as some specific challenges face educators in this realm.

AI literacy for educators and students

AI literacy is essential for both educators and students in today's rapidly advancing technological world. Developing AI literacy involves understanding AI concepts, staying up-to-date with current advancements, and applying AI tools effectively in various contexts. Here, we explore the ways in which educators and students at different levels can work on their AI literacy.

Elementary students:

For younger students, AI literacy focuses on introducing basic concepts and fostering curiosity. Educators can:

- Use age-appropriate resources, such as storybooks or animated videos, to explain AI concepts in simple terms.
- Encourage hands-on activities that involve programming simple robots or interacting with AI-powered tools and toys.
- Promote computational thinking and problem-solving skills through coding exercises and games.

Middle school students:

At the middle school level, AI literacy includes a deeper understanding of AI concepts and their applications. Educators can:

- Introduce more advanced AI concepts, such as machine learning and natural language processing, using interactive and engaging resources.
- Encourage students to experiment with AI tools, such as chatbots, to see how they work and understand their limitations.
- Foster discussions about the ethical implications of AI and the importance of responsible use.

High school students:

High school students should develop a comprehensive understanding of AI and its potential applications across various industries. Educators can:

- Offer elective courses or workshops focused on AI, covering topics like data science, machine learning, and robotics.
- Integrate AI tools and platforms into existing subjects, such as using AI-powered analytics in a statistics class or AI-generated art in a visual arts course.
- Guide students in undertaking AI-related projects or participating in AI competitions to apply their knowledge in real-world scenarios.

College students and adults:

At the college level and beyond, AI literacy involves specialized knowledge and staying current with the latest developments. Educators can:

- Offer advanced courses and seminars on AI, covering in-depth topics such as deep learning, reinforcement learning, and AI ethics.
- Facilitate interdisciplinary collaborations, enabling students to explore AI applications across different fields like healthcare, finance, and environmental science.
- Encourage students to attend conferences, workshops, and networking events to stay informed about industry trends and cutting-edge research.

For educators at all levels, it's crucial to stay informed about the latest AI advancements and best practices. They can:

- Participate in professional development programs and workshops focused on AI in education.
- Join online communities, forums, or social media groups dedicated to AI in education to share resources, experiences, and ideas.
- Subscribe to newsletters, journals, podcasts, and blogs that cover AI research, news, and trends.

By fostering AI literacy among both educators and students, we can ensure that they are well-equipped to navigate the rapidly changing landscape of AI in education and adapt their skills to the evolving demands of the future workforce.

The Role of Educators in Shaping the Future of AI

Educators play a crucial role in shaping the future of AI-driven education, and as such, they need to stay informed about AI advancements and develop their own AI literacy. Here are some more in-depth considerations for educators regarding AI literacy:

1. Understanding the fundamentals of AI:

Educators should have a solid grasp of AI's core concepts, such as machine learning, natural language processing, and neural networks. This understanding will enable them to effectively integrate AI tools into their teaching and explain these concepts to their students.

Educators can use resources such as online courses (e.g., Coursera, edX) and textbooks (e.g., "Artificial Intelligence: A Guide to Intelligent Systems" by Michael Negnevitsky) to develop a foundational understanding of AI concepts, including GPT technologies. They can introduce students to AI through projects like building simple chatbots or creating AI-generated art using GPT-powered tools like DALL-E.

2. Awareness of AI applications in education:

Educators should be familiar with various AI applications in the educational context, such as adaptive learning platforms, AI-powered tutoring systems, and automated grading tools. This awareness will help them better evaluate the potential benefits and drawbacks of using AI in their classrooms.

Educators should explore AI tools such as Quizlet (flashcards and study tools), Thinkster Math (AI-driven math tutoring), Brainly (AI-enhanced peer learning), and GPT-based AI like ChatGPT for generating writing prompts. They can integrate these tools into their lessons and encourage students to use them for self-directed learning.

3. Ethical considerations:

As AI becomes more prevalent in education, educators must be aware of ethical issues, such as data privacy, algorithmic bias, and the digital divide. They should be able to engage in meaningful discussions with students and colleagues about these issues and promote responsible AI use.

Educators can introduce ethics-focused lesson plans and activities, such as discussing the implications of AI-generated deepfakes or analyzing potential biases in GPT-driven language models. They can also use resources like the IEEE's Ethically Aligned Design framework to guide their understanding of AI ethics.

4. Pedagogical strategies for AI integration:

Educators should develop strategies for effectively incorporating AI tools into their lessons. This may involve using AI to enhance existing instructional methods or exploring new, innovative approaches to teaching with AI.

Educators can use AI tools like QuillBot to help students improve their writing or employ GPT-based AI like ChatGPT to generate creative writing prompts. They can also leverage AI-driven analytics to identify students' strengths and weaknesses, enabling personalized instruction.

5. Evaluating AI tools and resources:

As the market for AI-powered educational tools continues to grow, educators need to develop the skills to critically evaluate these tools, considering factors such as accuracy, user-friendliness, and potential biases. They should be able to determine which AI tools are best suited for their specific teaching goals and student needs.

Educators can consult expert reviews, user testimonials, and research studies to assess the effectiveness of AI tools, including GPT-powered applications. They can also pilot AI tools in their classrooms, gathering feedback from students and colleagues to determine the tools' suitability for their specific context.

6. Staying current with AI research and trends:

The field of AI is constantly evolving, and educators should stay informed about the latest developments in AI research, applications, and policy. This may involve reading academic journals, attending conferences and workshops, or participating in online forums and social media groups focused on AI in education.

Educators can subscribe to AI-focused newsletters, such as the AI Alignment Newsletter or the AI in Education Newsletter, and follow relevant organizations like AI4ALL or AI Now Institute on social media. They can also attend AI-related webinars, workshops, and conferences, such as the annual conference on Artificial Intelligence in Education, to stay informed about GPT advancements.

7. Collaborating with AI experts and researchers:

To deepen their understanding of AI, educators can benefit from collaborating with AI experts and researchers. This may involve partnering on research projects, inviting guest speakers to their classrooms, or participating in interdisciplinary initiatives that explore the intersection of AI and education.

Educators can reach out to local universities, AI research centers, or technology companies to establish connections with AI experts, including those specializing in GPT technologies. They can invite these experts to give guest lectures, collaborate on research projects, or serve as mentors for student-led AI initiatives.

8. Advocating for AI education:

Educators can play a key role in promoting AI literacy within their schools, districts, and professional networks. This may involve advocating for the inclusion of AI education in curricula, organizing AI-focused professional development opportunities, or sharing their own experiences and best practices with colleagues.

Educators can propose AI-focused courses, workshops, or extracurricular activities within their schools, emphasizing the importance of AI literacy for students' future success. They can also share their experiences with AI integration, including GPT-based tools, through blog posts, presentations at conferences, or webinars for fellow educators.

9. Developing a growth mindset:

Given the rapidly changing nature of AI, it's important for educators to maintain a growth mindset and be open to continuous learning. They should be willing to experiment with new AI tools and approaches, adapt their teaching methods as needed, and learn from both successes and failures.

Educators can model a growth mindset by engaging in ongoing professional development, experimenting with new AI tools like GPT-based systems, and reflecting on their experiences. They can also encourage students to embrace challenges, learn from failures, and view AI as a tool to support, rather than replace, learning efforts.

10. Preparing students for the future of work:

As AI continues to reshape the workforce, educators have a responsibility to prepare their students for the careers of the future. This involves not only teaching students about AI concepts and applications but also helping them develop essential skills like critical thinking, problem-solving, and adaptability, which will be crucial in an AI-driven world.

Educators can incorporate AI-related career exploration into their lessons, inviting guest speakers from various AI-driven industries, including those focused on GPT applications, or organizing field trips to AI-focused companies. They can also emphasize the importance of transferable skills like critical thinking, problem-solving, and adaptability, which will be valuable in an AI-driven job market.

By focusing on these aspects of AI literacy, educators can better prepare themselves and their students for the challenges and opportunities presented by AI in education.

Perspectives on The Future of AI in Education

Ms. Key and her friends walked out of the conference on The Future of AI in Education, buzzing with excitement and deep in thought. Each person had taken away something different from the event, and as they made their way to a nearby café to debrief, they eagerly shared their perspectives.

"I must admit, I'm still pretty skeptical about AI's role in education," said Mr. Adams, a seasoned educator known for his traditional teaching methods. "But I'm willing to keep an open mind and see where it leads us. It's hard to deny the potential benefits, especially when it comes to personalized learning."

Ms. Key, her eyes sparkling with enthusiasm, chimed in, "I'm all in! I can't wait to explore new ways to incorporate AI tools like GPT into my teaching. I think it can be a game-changer for both teachers and students if we use it responsibly and ethically."

Dr. Sanchez, a university professor, shared her concerns about the digital divide. "I think it's crucial that we ensure equal access to AI tools for all students, regardless of their socioeconomic backgrounds. We need to be proactive in bridging that gap to avoid perpetuating existing inequalities."

Ms. Patel, a tech-savvy educator, agreed. "Absolutely, and we also need to prepare our students for the careers of the future. By exposing them to AI concepts and tools early on, we're setting them up for success in a rapidly changing world."

As the group settled into their seats at the café, they continued to discuss the opportunities and challenges presented by AI in education. Each of them brought their unique perspectives, from cautious optimism to unbridled enthusiasm. Ms. Key was grateful for the lively debate, knowing that these conversations were essential to navigating the uncharted territory of AI-driven education.

With a steaming cup of coffee in her hands, Ms. Key couldn't help but feel hopeful. She knew that as long as educators like her friends and herself remained open-minded, adaptable, and committed to ethical practices, they could harness the power of AI to shape a brighter future for their students and society as a whole.

Ms. Key's Takeaways for AI in the Future of Education

Key Takeaway 1: AI will continue to play an increasingly significant role in shaping the future of education, making AI literacy essential for educators and students.

GPT Prompts:

a. How can educators prepare themselves and their students to embrace AI technologies in the classroom effectively?

b. What are some strategies for incorporating AI literacy into various curricula and grade levels?

c. How can teachers ensure that their students develop the skills needed to navigate an AI-driven world successfully?

d. In what ways can educators stay updated on the latest AI advancements and their applications in education?

e. What are some examples of AI literacy initiatives or programs that have successfully prepared students for the future?

Key Takeaway 2: Ensuring equal access to AI tools is vital in bridging the digital divide and promoting educational equity.

GPT Prompts:

a. What are some strategies for ensuring that all students have access to AI-enhanced learning opportunities?

b. How can educators and policymakers address the challenges of digital inequality in the context of AI in education?

c. What are some examples of initiatives or programs that have successfully promoted equal access to AI tools in education?

d. In what ways can partnerships between schools, governments, and the private sector help to bridge the digital divide?

e. How can educators incorporate discussions about digital inequality and AI access into their classrooms?

Key Takeaway 3: Teacher professional development in AI is crucial for the successful integration of AI tools in the classroom.

GPT Prompts:

a. What are some effective strategies for providing AI-focused professional development opportunities for educators?

b. How can schools and districts support teachers in acquiring the knowledge and skills needed to use AI tools effectively?

c. What are some examples of successful AI-focused professional development programs for educators?

d. In what ways can collaboration between educators, AI experts, and industry professionals enhance teacher training in AI?

e. How can educators advocate for increased investment in AI-focused professional development in their schools or districts?

Key Takeaway 4: Preparing students for careers in AI and related fields requires interdisciplinary learning and real-world experiences.

GPT Prompts:

a. What are some strategies for integrating AI-related concepts and skills across various subjects and curricula?

b. How can educators create opportunities for students to apply their AI knowledge and skills in real-world contexts?

c. What are some examples of projects or programs that have successfully prepared students for careers in AI and related fields?

d. In what ways can partnerships between schools and industry professionals expose students to AI career opportunities?

e. How can educators help students develop the soft skills needed to succeed in AI-related careers, such as teamwork and problem-solving?

Key Takeaway 5: The future of AI in education presents both opportunities and challenges that educators must navigate to ensure its positive impact.

GPT Prompts:

a. What are some potential benefits and drawbacks of increased AI integration in education?

b. How can educators balance the opportunities and challenges presented by AI to create meaningful learning experiences for their students?

c. What are some strategies for addressing concerns about privacy, ethics, and accountability in AI-enhanced education?

d. In what ways can educators promote responsible and ethical AI use among their students and colleagues?

e. What are some examples of successful AI-enhanced classroom experiences that have addressed potential challenges while maximizing opportunities?

Chapter 10

Envisioning the Future

E nvisioning the Future - Ms. Key's TED Talk

The stage lights shone brightly on Ms. Key as she walked up to the podium, her heart pounding with a mixture of excitement and nerves. She had been invited to give a TED Talk on her journey of embracing AI in education, and she was determined to inspire her fellow educators to explore the potential of AI in their classrooms.

"Ladies and gentlemen, fellow educators, and lifelong learners," she began, "today, I want to share my story with you—a story of curiosity, growth, and transformation. A story about how AI and tools like GPT have the power to revolutionize the way we teach and learn."

Ms. Key recounted her experiences throughout the school year, detailing her exploration of AI tools and their integration into her classroom. From using AI as a creative partner to pushing GPT to its creative limits, she shared her successes and challenges, and the impact on her students' learning experiences.

"As educators, our role is ever-changing, and we must adapt and evolve alongside the rapidly advancing world of technology," she continued. "AI has the potential to make education more engaging, personalized, and inclusive. However, we must always remember that AI should complement, not replace, our role as teachers. We must strive to maintain a balance between the human touch and AI assistance."

Ms. Key also addressed the importance of ethical considerations in using AI tools. "We have a responsibility to model ethical behavior and teach our students the importance of using AI responsibly. By fostering a culture of ethical decision-making, we can ensure that our students will use AI as a force for good in the world."

She encouraged her fellow educators to embrace a growth mindset and invest in their professional development. "Stay curious, keep learning, and collaborate with your peers to create innovative solutions for your students. The journey towards AI integration in education may seem daunting, but together, we can forge a path that embraces AI's potential while remaining grounded in the principles of effective teaching."

With an eye towards the future, Ms. Key painted a picture of a world where AI tools are seamlessly integrated into the classroom, enhancing learning experiences for all students. "Imagine a classroom where every student has access to personalized learning pathways, where educators can focus on fostering critical thinking and creativity, and where AI tools support and enhance our teaching methods."

As she concluded her talk, Ms. Key left her audience with a call to action. "Let us embrace this opportunity and embark on this exciting journey together, shaping the future of education with the power of AI. Our goal is not to replace the human touch but to enhance it, creating a more engaging and inclusive learning experience for our students."

The applause filled the auditorium as Ms. Key stepped down from the stage, her heart swelling with pride and hope. She knew her story had the power to inspire other educators to explore the potential of AI in their classrooms, and she was excited to see how this transformative technology would continue to shape the future of education.

As we come to the end of this incredible journey exploring the limitless potential of AI in education, I want to leave you with a sense of excitement and anticipation for the future. It's time to embrace GPT as our creative partner, to welcome this fantastic technology into our classrooms, and to embark on the adventure of a lifetime.

Throughout this book, we've discovered the immense power of GPT and AI to transform the way we teach and learn. From brainstorming sessions and project ideas to improving writing skills and nurturing critical thinking, GPT has proven itself to be an invaluable resource for educators and students alike.

Now, it's your turn to play, to experiment, and to have fun with GPT. Remember the importance of prompt engineering and asking the right questions. The more you interact with GPT, the better your understanding and relationship with this technology will become. So, dive in, and don't be afraid to make mistakes – that's how we learn and grow.

As you integrate GPT into your classroom, keep in mind the social-emotional benefits this technology can bring. By fostering collaboration, empathy, and communication skills, you'll be not only enhancing your students' learning experience but also preparing them for a future where AI-human collaboration is the norm.

I hope you've taken away from this book that GPT isn't just another cheating device, but an incredible tool for sparking a love of learning. By teaching students how to use GPT responsibly and creatively, you'll be empowering them to become lifelong learners and innovators. Embrace GPT's potential to enrich your curriculum, ignite your students' curiosity, and create a dynamic learning environment where both students and teachers can thrive.

We've also delved into the ways you can use GPT to streamline your teaching life, from lesson planning and organization to professional development and self-care. By leveraging GPT's capabilities, you can save time, reduce stress, and focus on what truly matters: inspiring your students and nurturing their growth.

As you embark on your GPTeacher journey, remember that you are not alone. Educators around the world are discovering the transformative power of AI in education. By sharing your experiences, challenges, and successes, you'll be contributing to the collective wisdom of this brave new world.

To help you get started, here are some simple steps to take as you begin your adventure with GPT:

1. Sign up for an account with OpenAI and familiarize yourself with ChatGPT.
2. Experiment with GPT on your own, learning its capabilities and limitations.
3. Begin incorporating GPT into your lesson planning and classroom activities.
4. Collaborate with other educators who are using GPT, sharing insights and ideas.
5. Reflect on your experiences, adjusting your approach as needed to optimize your use of GPT in the classroom.

In closing, let me extend my deepest gratitude for joining me on this journey. As a fellow educator and technology enthusiast, I am thrilled to be part of this exciting movement. I hope this book has inspired you to embrace AI as a creative partner and to harness its power to transform your classroom and teaching practice.

Now, go forth and explore the incredible world of GPTeacher. Embrace the unknown, face your fears, and let your creativity soar. Be open to the possibilities that GPT brings, and never forget that you are an essential part of this revolution in education.

I wish you the best of luck in your GPTeacher journey and look forward to hearing your stories of success, learning, and growth. Together, let's make a difference in the lives of our students and shape the future of education for generations to come.